Another Day, Another Collar

Another Day, Another Collar

Confessions of a dog trainer

Steve Mann

BLINK
bringing you closer

First published in the UK by Blink Publishing
An imprint of The Zaffre Publishing Group
A Bonnier Books UK Company
4th Floor, Victoria House,
Bloomsbury Square,
London, WC1B 4DA

Owned by Bonnier Books
Sveavägen 56, Stockholm, Sweden

Instagram: @blinkpublishing
X: @blinkpublishing

Hardback – 9781788705998
eBook – 9781788706001
Audio – 9781788708784

All rights reserved. No part of the publication may be reproduced, stored in a retrieval system, transmitted or circulated in any form or by any means, electronic, mechanical, photocopying, recording or otherwise, without prior permission in writing of the publisher.

A CIP catalogue of this book is available from the British Library.

Designed by Envy Designs Ltd
Printed and bound in Great Britain by Clays Ltd, Elcograf S.p.A.

1 3 5 7 9 10 8 6 4 2

Copyright © Steve Mann 2024

Steve Mann has asserted his moral right to be identified as the author of this Work in accordance with the Copyright, Designs and Patents Act 1988.

Every reasonable effort has been made to trace copyright holders of material reproduced in this book, but if any have been inadvertently overlooked the publishers would be glad to hear from them.

Blink Publishing is an imprint of Bonnier Books UK
www.bonnierbooks.co.uk

Dedicated to Alfa, the reason this book exists.
Legend.

Also by Steve Mann:

Easy Peasy Puppy Squeezy
Easy Peasy Doggy Squeezy
Easy Peasy Doggy Diary
Easy Peasy Awesome Pawsome
Easy Peasy Labrador
Easy Peasy Labradoodle
Easy Peasy Cocker Spaniel
Easy Peasy Cockapoo
Easy Peasy French Bulldog

Contents

Introduction   ix

1. The Greyhound   1
2. A Dog Named 'Dog'   21
3. Banjo   37
4. Alfa   59
5. Goat   77
6. Max   91
7. Woofy   101
8. Itzy   117
9. Amber   129
10. Chump   141
11. Alfa Animal Crew   159

12.	Nancy	175
13.	Maggie	191
14.	Lázaro	203
15.	Over Land and Sea	217
16.	Asbo	229
17.	Lucky	237
18.	Timing	251
	Acknowledgements	259

Introduction

I was seven years old when I first ate a flip-flop, on the drive home from Walton-on-the-Naze.

I was bored, I was curious and I wanted to know why dogs chewed shoes.

It felt amazing: a dopamine fix far exceeding the thrill of the seaside rollercoaster earlier in the day. Turns out the sole of a flip-flop is perfect for biting into, just like a banana is perfect for writing on with a ballpoint pen. Deeply satisfying. But here's the deal: you'll only know the pleasure if you do it yourself. (And, full disclosure, two hours later it didn't feel so great . . .)

When I was a kid, my dream was to spend as many hours as possible every day with dogs. My teachers at school told me to forget that. 'Dog trainer isn't a real job, Steve,' they said.

They weren't the only ones to be suspicious of my choice

of profession. I recently spent a morning training dogs in Hyde Park in London. After the session, covered in mud, I sat on a park bench with Pablo, my lovely old Staffie and best friend. I had my eyes closed and head tipped back to feel the warm sun on my face. I held my empty coffee cup in one hand and gently stroked Pablo's chest with the other. We were both in a very special place. A place of contentment. In that moment, we were genuinely as happy as we could possibly be.

After a while, I had that feeling of being watched. I opened my eyes and tilted my head forward to spot a woman and her two children looking at me. Our eyes met. 'Hello,' I said. She smiled kindly and replied 'Hi,' but as she spoke she quickly took her two kids by the hands and walked away. As they retreated, I heard her say to them, 'See! That's how you'll end up if you don't do what you're told!'

Sometimes, simply doing what you're told to do stops you from trying to understand.

Like everyone else, I could see that dogs behaved in certain ways. Unlike everyone else, I became obsessed with trying to understand that behaviour. My obsession led to a lifetime of pulling on the thread labelled 'Why?'.

Why *should* a dog behave the way we want them to?

Why *would* a dog behave the way we *don't* want them to?

I'm still pulling on that thread and I guess this book tells that story. It is not the type of memoir to go into granular

INTRODUCTION

detail. Rather, it's a series of stepping stones and signposts that show how I got from where I was to where I am, filtered through the lens of the dogs I've known and loved and my attempts to understand them. Each dog you'll read about has taught me many more lessons than I could ever teach them, but I've tried my best to return the favours. I hope that, in reading these stories, you too will find that by trying to understand our dogs, there's the potential to understand more about ourselves.

I should warn you, however, that if you take advice from someone who once ate a flip-flop, you'll get exactly what you deserve . . .

The Greyhound

I kind of hate myself for saying it, but I bloody adored going to Walthamstow dog track with my dad when I was a kid.

Like all of us, whether we admit it to ourselves or not, my dad was a gambler. I remember him telling me that he loved watching greyhounds race 'because they always try their best.' From as early as I can remember, I would accompany him most Saturday nights to the 'Stow.

Even the walk from the car to the huge art deco stadium was exciting, full of anticipation and completely unjustified optimism. *Welcome to Walthamstow Stadium, please leave all logic at the gate as you enter. Excuses, yeah-buts and if-onlys will be issued at the exit.* With a few lucky punts at the bookies, maybe Dad could turn the hot, sweaty ten-pence piece in my palm into a million pounds, enough to buy my very own greyhound. I was always transfixed by the huge floodlit statue of a beautiful black greyhound in full flight wearing the iconic red number one jacket.

Once through the turnstiles, Dad and I would go our separate ways. He'd turn left towards the bookies on the rails to check out the odds. I'd turn right and head over to the swings and slide to keep myself occupied before the racing began. I might only have been seven years old, but I was comfortable being on my own in a busy stadium.

ANOTHER DAY, ANOTHER COLLAR

Different times, I guess.

Once the dogs appeared, though, all my senses would spark into overdrive. The beauty of the racers, the pageantry of the 'huntsman' with his bowler hat and trumpet leading the procession, the stewards in white coats whose job it was to load the dogs into the traps as the lights went down in the grandstand, leaving only the illuminated halo of the track itself. In the moments before the race, there would be a mad rush and fighting to get to any bookie who had momentarily chalked the favourite at longer odds than the other bookies.

Then, a hush.

The steward in the white coat would wave towards the mechanical hare operator to signal that all six dogs were loaded into the traps. The trumpet fanfare would sound and the rattle of the mechanical hare would emanate from the far side of the stadium. As the punters craned their necks and dragged on their fags, I'd push my way between the sheepskin coats and down to the front to see the greyhounds crouched behind the bars in full predatory anticipation.

And then, as the hare passed . . . BANG!

The steward would pull the lever to open the traps and a huge roar would rise from the crowd as the dogs burst from their blocks and thundered towards the first bend. It was electric!

As soon as I'd watched the six dogs take the first bend, I'd sprint to the fourth bend, which they'd hit as they came up to the home straight. With my back to the track, I'd

THE GREYHOUND

close my eyes and listen to their feet thundering on the wet sand as lumps of the grit kicked up by the wide runners hit the back of my head and shoulders. *I touched the sand that touched the greyhound!* My Elvis used-towel moment.

One night at the races, I got lost, although I guess 'lost' is in the eye of the beholder. *I* knew exactly where I was, but my dad and the PA announcer were clearly not so confident. They found me at the back of the track, looking through the green iron bars to the kennels where the pre- and post-race dogs were kept on race night. To me, the kennel staff working there had the dream job. They would massage the competitors before putting on their racing jackets: the red number one, the blue number two, the black three on white, the white four on black, the black five on orange and – the very height of canine couture – the red number six on a black and white jacket for the wide runner. I was in trouble with Dad when he found me, but not half as much trouble as he'd have been in with Mum if he hadn't . . .

When the race was done, and a fresh cohort of dogs filed into the lights of the Cockney Coliseum for their pre-race parade, the spent post-racers would pass them at the gate, their mouths wide open, their tongues hanging and – what struck me most – steam rising from their bodies like smoke from a spent shotgun cartridge. The kennel hand would weigh the dogs in front of the steward, then give them a big metal bucket of water to drink as they cleaned the sand off their feet like blacksmiths shoeing a horse, dry

ANOTHER DAY, ANOTHER COLLAR

them with a towel and wrap them in a big fleece jacket to keep them warm. With all this going on, never once did the dog come up for air from their bucket of water.

When each race was over, they would display the actual photo of the finish, snapped as the dogs crossed the line, in a wall-mounted glass display case. These photos were taken to support the results that were announced over the Tannoy, prior to the bookies paying out on the winning tickets. I guess they were displayed in case anyone had a gripe with the announced results. An effort at full transparency. (Yeah, right – because the greyhound racing industry is as pure as the driven snow.) As one race finished and the corresponding photo was exhibited, the photo of the previous race was taken down and thrown to the floor along with a million fag butts and a billion better-luck-next-time-my-wife's-gonna-kill-me scrunched-up betting slips. I couldn't believe my luck each night as I sneaked out of the stadium with a dozen greyhound photos tucked under my parka. Back home, my bedroom walls were covered in those black-and-white pictures of greyhound race photo-finishes. No Bruce Lee or A-Team posters for me. Why would I want those, when I could have Lacca Champion pipping Tartan Khan by a short head?

When the last race was run, as punters were streaming out of the stadium late on Saturday night, newspapermen would be selling the Sunday papers out of the back of their vans. This Marty McFly voodoo blew my mind each week. If only they sold those papers a little earlier in the evening, we could have looked up who'd won the last race before it was run. We could have been millionaires, Rodney!

If Dad had done well with the 'bow-wows', he'd buy me a bag of monkey nuts from the 'PEEEEEENUUUTS!!' man who famously roared his wares. I could gauge my chances of getting a bag of peanuts by the pace at which Dad exited the stadium. If things had gone well, we'd saunter leisurely back. If they hadn't, Dad's adrenaline would be up so the walk back to the car occurred at a fierce rate, Dad forging ahead with me jogging fifty paces behind, trying to keep up. Safe to say, I rarely got the chance to develop a peanut allergy.

I still sometimes drive past Walthamstow dog stadium. The track is long gone, with the bulk of the site now a residential housing area. But its listed-building status means that elements of the old stadium and entrance remain in place.

A lot of my childhood memories are wrapped up in that place. I'd often skip school to visit the track and watch the daytime races, as at the time I often felt more comfortable in the company of dogs than humans. I'm reminded of Charlie Chan's, the nightclub under the stadium, where the hoi polloi of east London used to hang out. My mates and I would sometimes sneak into Charlie Chans while we were still underage. My mate Kevin was once even attacked by the bouncers as he was falsely accused of passing fake

£50 notes over the bar. (Although, frankly, if we'd ever thought Kev had fifty quid in his pocket, we'd probably have attacked him ourselves.)

Back then, my innocence allowed me only to see the excitement and beauty of a night at the races. In my teenage years, I used to go to the track on Tuesdays, Thursdays and Saturdays. Not to gamble, but to see the dogs and to flesh out my dreams. As I grew older, however, I began to see greyhound racing for what it was: an industry where the dogs never came first. Sometimes I miss the naivety that allowed me to enjoy those nights, but in the final analysis, dog racing presented far too many unanswered or poorly answered welfare questions for me to feel it should ever have a place in society.

So to pass the stadium nowadays is bittersweet. I guess it'll just have to be okay to appreciate the ruins of the coliseum, as long as we can also spare a prayer for the gladiators.

My dad died in 2005 at the age of sixty-seven. Later, as a man in my thirties with a wife and son of my own, I had a burning desire to welcome one of those gladiators into our home. I've no doubt that subconsciously I was harking back decades and trying to cling on to what I could of my dad. I had a gap in my life, and it was greyhound shaped.

Over the years, I had often headed over to the kennels for retired racing greyhounds in Waltham Abbey to do what I could. Lots of kind volunteers would donate their time to look after these dogs, some of whom were battered and bruised after a life of racing, others had retired early through lack of performance or turning a profit. Many people would have seen nothing but kennel after kennel of unwanted dogs. For me, it was more a retirement home for rock stars. I'd donate dog food, offer my training services or simply walk some of these beauties around the nearby paddocks.

One day, I pulled up outside the kennels in my van and before I could even exit the vehicle, Jane, the kennels manager, came over. She belted out her usual joke. 'Come to take one home this time, have you?'

I rolled down my van window and, with the air of a cocky Harry Redknapp on transfer deadline day, said, 'Actually, yeah.'

Jane laughed. 'Sure. What are you really up here for?'

'Seriously, I'm in the market for a greyhound, Jane.'

'Blimey.' She didn't give me a chance to back-pedal. 'You'd better come on in and have a look at what we've got.'

I shook my head. 'I'll tell you what, Jane. I'm going to stay put while you go on in and choose the one that deserves a new start. Grab the one that's been with you the longest. Male or female, I don't mind.'

'You sure?' said Jane. 'Could be a handful, you know?'

She was right about that. These dogs are bred to be super-high drive and chase anything that moves. As young dogs, these greyhounds might only have been exposed to a kennel, the back of a van and a race track – they'd never seen traffic, TVs or children, which can often lead to issues on civvy street. But before I could change my mind, she dashed into the kennel block and came out with an absolute beauty who pranced ahead of the tight lead, looking more stallion than dog.

Unable to take my eyes off this stunner, I got out of my van to greet him and asked the obligatory first question when meeting a new dog for the first time. 'What's his name?'

'This is Johnny Sit,' said Jane.

'Johnny what?'

'Johnny Sit.'

Now, racing greyhounds will have two or three different names. The first is the litter name from their official pedigree paperwork. The second is the name that appears on the race-track programme and the bookies' chalkboards. These are zany names like Wagamamas Woo-Woo or La-La-Land Larry Loopy Loo. The third name is what's referred to as their kennel name, which is the nickname used by the kennel staff on a day-to-day basis.

Even the most successful racing greyhounds will have a super-short career. If they manage to stay in one piece, they're generally considered by the 'industry' to be past their best at around four years of age. The next ten years can be a very unpredictable period for each dog, once they're considered, mercenarily, as surplus to requirements. Johnny Sit had retired at the ripe old age of three and spent the next two years at the rescue kennels. There had been a couple of rehoming attempts, but he had bounced back to the kennels very quickly each time because he was – as Jane euphemistically said – 'a bit of a handful'.

He had gained his kennel moniker of Johnny Sit after a famous incident that took place the first time he was taken to Walthamstow dog track to be 'graded'. When a new dog is registered at a track, they need to run a grading race so they can have a time recorded against their name, with the fastest dogs graded A1 and the slowest graded A10. The racing manager can then group dogs of a similar ability to race each other. The racing style of the dogs will also be considered. Do they naturally run wide in pursuit of the hare? If so, they would be 'wide dogs' and drawn in traps five or six. Perhaps they 'hug the rails' when they race? If so, they'd spring from traps one or two, the 'inside' draw. Gradings are sometimes run solo, sometimes with two or three other dogs, in an empty stadium. This was often only witnessed by a few owners, trainers and track officials (and a kid called Stephen John Patrick Mann who should have been at school but wasn't missed).

The legend goes that for his grading, my dog had been loaded into the traps along with two other debutants. As the hare passed and the traps exploded open, all three flew out and raced to the first bend. All was as it should be. By the second bend, however, Jonny was not so much chasing a hare as smelling a rat. He slowed to a jog, then to a walk and, by the third bend, to a sit. A sit?!

The other two dogs continued in hot pursuit of the hare

while Johnny remained a polite observer. He looked back over one shoulder, then the other, watching the racers circle him while his butt never left the sand. If you know greyhounds, you'll be aware that because of their body shape and mechanics, they almost never choose to sit. Yet this fella's butt was glued to the spot like a Just Stop Oil protestor.

The graders had never seen this happen. A record-breaking greyhound. This guy was for me. I love the special ones!

Back home, I unloaded Johnny Sit from the van and spent a little time with him lying under a tree. After a while, I let our other dogs – Pablo the Staffie, Zeta and Itzy the German shepherds – out of the house to meet him and, following a few half-hearted butt-sniffs, Johnny strolled past the other dogs, through the front door, through the hall, into the living room and melted onto our settee. He remained there for most of the following eight years.

As a family, we decided that this day was to be the first day of the rest of his life. We wanted to swipe the old Etch-a-Sketch as clean as possible, which meant giving him a new name. (Not to mention that I dreaded the thought of having to explain his old name of 'Johnny Sit' a million times in the future.) When I was a boy, I used to dream up imaginary names for imaginary dogs that lived in my imaginary house. So I gave my son Luke, who was seven at the time, the honour. (And oh my days, what an honour it is to name a dog.) Luke was – and remains – a real football nut. 'His name,' he said, without missing a beat, 'is to be Pele.'

'Awesome!'

'Pele Longsocks, to be exact,' said Luke.

'Ah, okay. Pele Longsocks it is.'

Pele Longsocks slotted in with my other dogs like he'd lived with them all his life. In true greyhound style, he would lounge and sleep for twenty-three-and-a-half hours a day, with the remaining half hour dedicated to ablutions, a look outside the front door just to make sure the world was still there, and sixty seconds allocated to the zoomies.

You know what I mean by the zoomies, right?

The zoomies – or FRAPS (frenetic random activity periods) to give them their scientific name – are something most dogs will do, particularly when they're young. All of a sudden, and quite apropos of nothing, they will decide to run around like their tail is on fire. As they run, they assume this weird maniacal position which makes it look like their back legs are running faster than their front legs. Their look of delight as they watch their butts flying past in their wing mirrors is a joy to behold.

Most dogs look ridiculous when the zoomies hit. Pele, however, enjoyed the most elegant of zoomies, like Nijinsky on a jet ski or a body-popping Cary Grant. The patterns he traced looked completely random. However, my suspicion was that if we watched him from above and followed the jet-stream trail he left, we would have seen that he was writing out the words 'I love bread'.

ANOTHER DAY, ANOTHER COLLAR

Because Pele, perfect Pele, had but one vice. He was obsessed with bread. He would rush up to every visitor expectant, eyes glistening, as if to say, 'Are you bread? Are you *bread*? Are you *made* of bread? Do you *have* bread? Have you *heard* of bread? *OMG, bread's amazing!*' Every bag, every pocket, every nook and every cranny was explored with a nose that had clearly been selectively bred for many generations to explore every such bag, pocket, nook and cranny . . . for bread. No sandwich within a five-mile radius of Pele was safe and it was often only the promise of a pinch of Hovis that could stir him from the couch.

Pele's particular tastes were not surprising when you considered his history. The rescue kennels where he stayed for two years often relied on whatever food donations came their way just to keep their dogs going. Donated kibble, trays of out-of-date Pot Noodles, porridge and stale old bread would be tipped into a big bathtub, covered in boiling water and served up like a Victorian gruel. But things were going to be different for Pele from now on.

In training, I only needed to focus on improving one behaviour in order to keep Pele on the straight and narrow. It was a simple thing, but an important one all the same: Stop. Trying. To. Kill. Little. Dogs.

My early walks with Pele were a sheer pleasure, until he saw a small dog, such as a shitzu or Lhasa apso. It was then that the 'stallion' I first saw exiting the rescue kennels with Jane reappeared. He'd rear up – or, more commonly,

THE GREYHOUND

'Pele Longsocks'

revert to his track days and bend his front end down, chin to the ground, waiting for the hare to pass and the traps to open. Thankfully, he was always on lead to prevent him from doing a different kind of porridge, m'lud.

As an apprentice dog trainer, I often heard my elders say, 'If it's in the dog, it'll come out of the dog.' They meant that if a particular breed had been subjected to a very specific and focused selective breeding programme to emphasise a certain desired trait, rather than working against the dog to try to suppress that trait, a happier, smoother and mutually beneficial attitude to take in training is to satisfy that desire, but on your own safer

ANOTHER DAY, ANOTHER COLLAR

and more socially acceptable terms. (A good lesson there, I think, for teachers, parents and managers.)

Well, I knew that Pele had a huge hunger for chasing and grabbing little furry dogs. So every day I would go out into my garden with a tea towel and, when he looked at me, I would shout, 'Get it!' and throw the tea towel for him to chase. Or I'd run backwards to enable him to chase me over a short distance, and grab and 'kill' the tea towel with me. That was our first stage. I wanted Pele to know that if he felt the urge to chase and grab, he could simply look to me and I would offer him that outlet, safely.

The next stage was to head outside with the tea towel and, when a small dog appeared, I would say, 'Get it!' jog back a little bit and let Pele satisfy his predatory urges by playing with me and the tea towel. With enough repetition, whenever he saw a small dog, Pele would feel that fire in his belly and understand it as his cue to look at me. And when Pele looked at me, that was my cue to pull out the tea towel and pop it in his mouth. This meant that he was already holding the 'rabbit'. No dog in their right mind will chase a rabbit if they're already holding a rabbit. A bird in the mush is worth two in the bush. Everyone was happy and no one was harmed.

Pele was also prone to what we called 'hot laps'. Now and then, whenever the fancy took him, he would start flying around in the kitchen: over chairs, under tables, even around the walls like Evel Knievel. Sometimes he would fancy some hot laps at four in the morning. Of course he bloody would! He'd been sleeping the vast majority of the previous day! Woken by thundering paws downstairs at 4am, I would grumpily creep out of bed, descending the stairs with squinted eyes. When I got to the bottom, however, I would witness the joy of Pele grinning at me, tongue lolling, as if to say, 'Oh my God, this is amazing! We're alive! We're alive! Come on, Dad, jump on in, this is amazing!'

I couldn't help but love him.

And I couldn't help but learn from him, as we all should try to learn from our dogs.

One night at the 'Stow when I was in my early teens, an old Crombie-coated pearly sage told me how amazing it was that a winning greyhound had the know-how to hold back until the final bend, before going full pelt for glory and winning the race. Like Ovett cunningly sitting on Coe's shoulder.

It was nonsense, of course. Sportingly romantic nonsense, but nonsense all the same. What the old boy saw through his rose-tinted glasses was not one dog speeding up at the end but five other dogs slowing down. Greyhounds neither know nor care that they're in a 475-, 640- or 820-metre race. They don't time their run accordingly. Greyhounds don't race, they chase. It's not a group event but an individual pursuit, as far as they're concerned. The successful dogs don't look to hurt the others, but they don't get out of their way either. They don't even see the other dogs when in the flow. That would be a waste of time and energy. Their competitors are none of their business. They don't consider the distance or their own limitations. They don't adjust and pivot to what others are doing. They focus with 100 per cent effort from the get-go. And, win or lose, you'll never hear a greyhound offer excuses in a post-race interview.

Welcome to the Steve Mann School of Business.

When I first started my business, I was repeatedly told to research what other professional dog trainers were charging for their classes and to pitch my tent accordingly. I was told that I should teach this way or that because that's how the clients' previous trainers taught them. It didn't make sense to me. Why charge the same and do the same? So I could sit comfortably within the bunch?

I'd never catch the mechanical hare that way.

I don't want to be a sled-pulling husky, in business or in life. I want to be a greyhound. If I'm going to do something, I'm going to do it 100 per cent. I might never be the most skilled or accomplished, but I'm prepared to be the most committed and won't be affected by what others are doing, what others are charging or what others are saying. They're none of my business. And, like the greyhound, I'll also never offer excuses in a post-race interview.

I go all in, whether I'm developing new courses, building a business or committing to helping a dog. But don't get me wrong – this approach also holds for relaxing. If I'm

THE GREYHOUND

going to do nothing, I'm going be King Lazy of Slobdom, just like the greyhound. Chair reclined, feet up, fourth movie of the day on TV, smothered in sleeping dogs and a bag of crisps big enough to choke a donkey.

Greyhounds taught me that if you're going to do something, do it! Don't even acknowledge those naysayers who line up around you to say, 'Yeah, but . . .'

Yeah, but you're too young to train other people's dogs.

Yeah, but your type don't build their own businesses.

Yeah, but you can't lie on the settee all day.

Yeah, but you can't run around the kitchen at 4am with your tongue hanging out, purely for joy.

Yeah, but you can't hope that everything is made of bread.

Turns out you can. And you should. Whether you're chasing a goal, relaxing, eating, caring or working – how you do anything is how you do everything. Finding balance to me isn't about trying to manage 40 per cent of life with one hand, 35 per cent of life with the other hand and 25 per cent of life precariously teetering on my head. Like the greyhound, I find my balance by focusing 100 per cent on one thing. Then, when I'm ready, I put that down and focus on the next thing, 100 per cent.

A spoiler alert, though, for the fellow greyhounds out there: no one ever catches the mechanical hare. But the way I see it, the greyhound is in ecstasy while he's running, not once he's finished. And who in their right mind wants to get to the end of their race anyway?

ANOTHER DAY, ANOTHER COLLAR

Good old Pele Longsocks lived to the ripe old age of twelve before he succumbed to cancer.

I was training dogs and handlers abroad when we got the call from the Royal Veterinary College to let us know it was time to say goodbye. I flew home early. I sat with him on the surgery floor and loaded slice after slice of bread into his grinning mouth while the vet did what she had to do. Pele couldn't have been happier in that moment, and we couldn't have been more heartbroken.

Despite being born as nothing more than a commodity into the seedy betting industry, Pele had the beauty and grace to live purely for joy alone. He never spared a thought for the settee when he was chasing, and he never spared a thought for chasing when he was on the settee. He woke up like a bird at 4am, dancing and singing because he couldn't believe how lucky he was to have been gifted another lap.

A Dog Named 'Dog'

I feel the lessons learned from Pele not so much in my head, but in my heart and my gut.

I'm sure the most memorable lessons are viscerally anchored. Something you can hear or see, sure, but also something you can *feel*. You'll always remember the details of the movies that cheered you up, filled you with tension or scared the living daylights out of you. The song lyrics you recall won't necessarily be from a particularly 'good' song, but from a song that's intrinsically linked to a memory or emotion.

Lessons are at their most adhesive when they're paired with feelings. Good teachers know this.

Mrs Jakubac was a good teacher.

My academic career could best be described as 'hit and miss'. Like Pele the greyhound, I only had two settings: all-in or all-out. And like any dog, if somebody wanted me to do something, I'd ask myself, 'Why should I? What's the benefit to me?' It's a perfectly fair question as far as I'm concerned. And an unfair reply to that question is, 'Because I told you so.'

'Because I told you so' isn't decent teaching in any school, be it a school for children or a school for dogs. At its best, that reply is merely stewarding. At its worst, it's bullying.

For me, benefits beat bullying every time.

ANOTHER DAY, ANOTHER COLLAR

Whenever there was a school parents' evening and the feedback from the teacher wasn't *too* disastrous, my dad would leave a five pence in my school desk for me to find the next day so I could buy a packet of crisps at break. In winter term 1978, though, when I was eight years old, there was no five pence to be found because the feedback that term was particularly disastrous. With her head in her hands, Mrs Jakubac admitted to my mum and dad that she didn't know what to do with me in class because I was so disruptive. 'He has no interest in the syllabus. There's just far too much chatting about dogs and football. He's *obsessed*.' (It was almost as if she thought being obsessed was a bad thing.)

Mum was clean out of carrots that night, but she had plenty of stick to try. Her suggestion was sharp and to the point. 'Well, take him off the football team. He'll soon learn.'

Mrs Jakubac also happened to be coach of our school football team. The suggestion horrified her. 'I can't do that,' she said. 'He's our best player!'

And so she came up with a much more elegant plan.

Next day in class, we were told we could sit anywhere we wanted to, as long as it wasn't in a place we had sat previously that week. This not only provided a sneaky shift of environment to stop me whispering to my usual accomplices, it also offered a little spark of novelty to engage me. Learners love novelty in their lessons, and in later life, I would use Mrs Jakubac's technique in my own classes. I realised that if I had bog standard cones and poles out for my group dog training classes, it's the same old, same old. So I became a bit of a skip rat and would pilfer gnomes, mannequins and all manner of curiosities. When the class enters the field to see an army of gnomes to navigate around rather than boring old cones, believe me, it's a game changer. It piques their interests and engages them, so they're ready to listen and learn before the lesson even begins.

It couldn't all be novelty, though. Mrs Jakubac had a syllabus for us to follow. Happily for me, she pitched it to us just right. We all had to do a 'project' by the end of term. Rather than telling us what the topic had to be, she released us into the 'library' (a cardboard box containing about thirty second-hand books) and allowed us to pick out any book we fancied, so we could choose our own topic, rather than being forced to study something we couldn't see the point of. There were no decent dog books in the box – this was thirty-eight years before the Steve Mann *Easy Peasy* dog training book revolution) – so I chose a book about the Olympics and set to work.

The 'project' was, really, like any other piece of schoolwork, but we were allowed to do it in larger books with pages that smelled of bran. As we read, glued and copied into our project books, Mrs Jakubac stood poised for a generous distribution of her coveted gold stars. In my hunt for gold stars, I picked the low-hanging fruit first by decorating my project book with a drawing of the five Olympic rings. Having safely bagged a gold star for that, I went looking for more of the good stuff. I discovered that the five rings symbolise the union of the five continents. I went on to read about Cassius Clay . . . which led me to read about why he changed his name to Muhammad Ali . . . which led to me learning about his role in the civil rights movement . . . which led to me learning about Vietnam. From Vietnam, I jumped to the Black Panthers . . . to the Black Power salute . . . to Malcolm X. And I'd researched all that before my morning milk.

Mrs Jakubac didn't teach me about the Olympics. She taught me *how to learn* about the Olympics. Give a Mann a fish and all that. In doing this, she also gave me important lessons not just in learning, but in teaching. I use those lessons in dog training all the time:

- To minimise unwanted behaviour, change the environment where the unwanted behaviour previously occurred.
- Choice gives the learner agency, ownership and pride.
- Gold stars, either metaphorical or real, illustrate the value of reinforcement. If you see a behaviour you want more of, you'd better make sure it gets reinforced or you may be waiting a long time to see it again.
- Make learning fun.

The following year, when I was nine, my teacher was cool Mr Kavanagh. He, thankfully, always appreciated that teaching is not just stewarding. Whereas the other class in our year was nailed rigidly to the syllabus and to their books to learn about poetry, Mr Kavanagh took us on a magical mystery tour to arrive at the same destination. To do this, he brought in a record player.

A record player! The class was so excited he might as well have brought in a bazooka or a lion. There was no 'Macavity: The Mystery Cat' for us. *We* got to listen to a Roxy Music album instead. Like Mrs Jakubac had done, Mr Kavanagh added the magnetic ingredient of novelty to his teaching. He chalked the Roxy Music lyrics on the blackboard and encouraged us to change them to make up our own unique song. With our own words in place, he removed the musical scaffolding to reveal that each of us had written our own personal poem. If only Brian Ferry had tried a little harder, he too could have written 'Love Is the Dog' instead of 'Love Is the Drug'. Shame.

For homework, we had to create a poem of our own about a subject we loved, to the tune of another hit song. I was issued Elton John's 'Daniel' as inspiration.

> My spaniel is travelling tonight on a plane
> I can see his tail wagging, wanting a game
> And I see my spaniel, he's a good boy
> Oh it looks like my spaniel
> Chasing the ball and chewing his toy

To us nine-year-olds, this felt like the birth of rock and roll. So cheers, Mr K. Nice one.

ANOTHER DAY, ANOTHER COLLAR

It wasn't all gravy, though. I became the victim of my own success by being a bit of a star in Mr Kavanagh's cross-country team. I hated cross-country running. It kept me away from football and dog training at the weekends, and it was only the fear of losing, not the joy of winning, that kept me putting one cold, wet, muddy foot in front of the other. However, a lesson was there to be learned in how we define strengths and weaknesses.

In my opinion, and contrary to popular belief, a strength isn't necessarily something you're good at. It *can* be, of course, but what it *must* be is something that gives you joy, energy and ambition. It needs to be something that you look forward to and want to think about before you go to sleep or first thing in the morning when you wake up. Dog training was that for me when I was younger and, believe me, when I was younger, I was a terrible dog trainer. That didn't mean it wasn't a strength of mine, though.

On the flip side, I was great at cross country. But it made me nervous, I dreaded it when going to sleep and, even though I could run all day long, it drained me mentally and stopped me doing what I truly wanted to do. For me, cross country was a weakness.

Being good at something isn't enough. My advice is to do loads of whatever you look forward to, whether you're good at it or not. The irony is that if you keep turning up and doing enough of it, you can't help but get good at it. The rule for me is this: if you feel it in your heart, do it more; if you feel it in your belly, do it less. Just as a

A DOG NAMED 'DOG'

whippet is bred to chase and a husky is bred to pull, we're much better when we play the cards we're dealt.

I liked my junior school. I learned loads. Admittedly, what I learned was not always what the teachers set out to teach. (Muhammad Ali, Malcom X, Roxy Music . . . who needs Pythagoras?) But I learned *how* to learn and, more importantly, I learned how to teach. Mrs Jakubac and Mr Kavanagh taught me how controlling the environment, novelty, choice and celebrating small wins sets the learner (and the teacher) on the right path. Thanks Mrs J and Mr K. I owe you one.

Which is more than I can say for Mr Harold, the headmaster, who, after I had quit the cross-country team, choose assembly as a good time to embarrass me in front of the whole school when I mispronounced his name. 'It's not "Mr *Arold*", is it, boy?' he said in a stupid voice. 'Learn to speak properly. Don't drop your Hs.' That dig sat in my belly and kept me awake for weeks.

Brace yourself now for a sharp left turn and a big reveal. I bet it had never crossed your mind that I might have spent time in jail?

Well, think again. I have. A few stretches, in fact.

Admittedly those stretches only lasted four to six hours each, but let the record show – *squints off into the distance as he draws on a cigarette* – I've done bird.

I've been involved in several projects that have paired

up rescue dogs with inmates of different prisons and young offender institutions to give them an opportunity to teach, care and learn. In addition to the dog training sessions I led, the projects also included each carer being responsible for the dog's welfare, feeding, exercise and emotional wellbeing.

The first jail I visited was just outside Glasgow. I was checked by security and relieved of my usual teaching paraphernalia. I was allowed no laptop, no USBs, no pens. Zilch!

'What can I bring in?' I asked the guard.

'You can use what the rest of us rely on, son. Your wits.'

'What about my shiv or snout?' I asked in my best Ray Winstone voice, in an effort to break the ice.

The ice remained intact. If anything, it was thicker.

Once inside the jail, matters were different. I've found these projects gave the inmates a real sense of purpose. Some of them may have missed out on early school life, and I found that my own early experiences with Mrs Jakubac and Mr Kavanagh were of real value in such situations. When a tutor sat them in a classroom and said they needed to learn basic maths, they'd often reply, 'Why should I?' When we bypassed the sterile classroom, however, and let them know they needed to order enough food for Bella, who would eat 250g of food twice a day for the next nine days, it was a different matter. Bella was in their care and they genuinely did *care* for her. It meant they'd do the maths and call in the order so Bella's food was delivered in time. If each guardian had the responsibility to keep a daily training log for the dog in their care, they'd practise their reading and writing. They might also be asked to produce a training manual for the new owners, should the rescue dog in their care be lucky enough to find a forever home on the outside.

A lot of these guys never lasted the academic distance as kids due to their upbringing and environment. The rescue dog projects helped to load these skills with a real-life purpose, via a topic that they were interested in and cared about. Why should I? Bella, mate, that's why.

These institutions are interesting places. I found that each rescue dog programme I ran included a group of guys who clearly 'went along' with the plans of others on the wrong side of the law. I fear they always will and are destined to bounce in and out of custodial sentences forever. However, others on the course were as sharp and as smart as anybody I've ever met, in any environment. They were constantly looking for, and often finding, angles and inside tracks to give them an advantage, from workloads to punchlines. I loved how these calculations were created and executed. Put these entrepreneurs on the right side of the tracks in a different environment and you've got yourself market leaders, Lord Sugar.

I ran a few dog rescue projects in a heavier prison in Ireland, where all the dogs on the course were paired up with lifers. None of these blokes could expect to leave prison for a good twenty years and, although I was justifiably pooping myself the first time I stood in front of them, many of the prisoners oddly didn't seem to have a care in the world. They were cheerful, interested, helpful, relaxed and enthusiastic about the project. Of course, come midnight and they're in their cell with nothing but their demons for company and I'm sure things were different. But on the dog course, they were honestly a joy. That's the beauty of interacting with dogs: when you're with them, and training them, you think of nothing else.

The key to getting these students to apply themselves to their maths, reading and writing was to find the correct conduit for these lessons, just as Mrs Jakubac did for me more than forty years ago. The correct conduit, as is often the case, was dogs. Through dogs, we could answer the 'why' question. Through dogs, we had an anchoring emotion. Through dogs, we were able to change the environment.

🐾

Another person at school taught me an important technique to help embed lessons into the brain for good. 'Make 'em laugh, you're halfway there,' as Michael Caine almost said in *Alfie*. And although his character had sneakier aspirations, the tool is just as potent if you want your lessons to stick.

If something is interesting, I'll *want* to remember it. If something is valuable, I'll *try* to remember it. But if something is funny, I'll *definitely* remember it . . . forever.

I'm willing to bet you're the same. So, with this in mind,

ladies and gentlemen, meet my fellow eight-year-old pupil from 1979, Chris Persimmon.

We were in the playground during morning break one day. Think tennis balls, skipping ropes, stones, spit, fists and fizzing hormones. Just as playtime was coming to an end, what should we see but a crazed dog with wide eyes and a foaming mouth belting around the playground with a hundred kids – eyes even wider, mouths even foamier – shrieking in hot pursuit. Out came the teacher with a big bell like a town crier and, as rehearsed a thousand times previously, upon its toll all the kids froze like statues. Pavlov's children.

We watched Mrs Reynolds trying to catch the dog, yelling what I thought was a hell of a long-shot guess at the stray's name – 'Dog! *Dog!*' she cried – to the backdrop of kids absolutely pissing themselves. I took a chance and started doing star jumps to grab the dog's attention. When the dog looked at me curiously, I bent down and pretended to investigate an imaginary object on the floor. It was a cunning plan, of course, to attract the dog.

As the dog came over to me, I gently held his collar and normal service was resumed. A fuming Mrs Reynolds took the dog, looped a skipping rope through his collar as a makeshift lead and marched him to the headmaster's office, the way all playground villains were marched. Pavlov's teacher. I like to think they asked the school secretary to call the dog's parents.

Back in the playground, Mrs Reynolds yelled at us all. 'He's a naughty dog and you're all naughty children!'

ANOTHER DAY, ANOTHER COLLAR

There's a quote from B. F. Skinner, author of *The Behaviour of Organisms*, that I love: 'The rat is always right.' Skinner had got angry with certain rats during his laboratory studies. He had developed particular predictive theories on how the rats would respond to a reinforcement structure he had set up. However, time and time again, the rats responded and behaved unexpectedly. Annoyed, Skinner blamed the rats for their disobedience. Minutes later, having realised that being annoyed at the rats was preposterous, it dawned on him that the rat is always right. The rat will behave like a rat and, given their experience and the information they have at the time, will act in the way that is right for them at that moment.

It's not a naughty rat.

It's not a disobedient rat.

It's not a dominant rat.

It's just a rat.

And the dog was just a dog. And we kids were just kids, behaving as kids do.

As the dust settled in the playground, fun turned to fear as all us kids were lined up to be told that no one was allowed back in the school until the person who had opened the school gate to let the dog in owned up.

All eyes turned to Chris Persimmon.

Chris was one of the funniest characters you could ever hope to meet, but completely on his own frequency. Mrs Reynolds approached him. 'Did you let the dog into the playground?'

A DOG NAMED 'DOG'

'No, Miss.'
'Did you let the dog into the playground?'
'No, Miss.'
'Did you let the dog into the playground?'
'I don't know, Miss.'
'Did you let the dog into the playground?'
'Yes, Miss.'
'Why did you let the dog into the playground?'
'Because I thought it was a log.'

A log?

There is a scene in the movie *Escape to Victory* where the prisoners nervously line up in silence for inspection with a mannequin in their ranks to cover for their mate who got out over the wall the previous night. The mannequin's head falls off and the prisoners' silence segues into roars of delight at the sheer preposterousness of it all.

Well, that.

Man, I love the human condition. We're so ridiculous when put under pressure. Our heart rate goes haywire and our brain's usually coherent signal becomes chaotic. As soon as we're into fight or flight, the game's over. We essentially cut off the blood flow to our processing systems, giving ourselves a DIY frontal lobotomy and causing us to blurt out the most ridiculous statements. That's why Chris went with 'log' when challenged. Classic monkey brain.

'Why would you open the gate to let a log into the playground, Chris?' Mrs Reynolds demanded.

'I don't know, Miss.'

ANOTHER DAY, ANOTHER COLLAR

Nice one, Chris; they can't argue with surrealism.

It made me laugh so much that the whole incident is laser engrained into my DNA. I reckon in generations to come, my great, great, great, great grandchildren will instinctively laugh at logs and not know why. That's epigenetics, that is.

I learned three things that day: dogs will behave like dogs, pressure makes people do crazy things and if you can make people laugh, they'll remember. It's something I try to do with my teaching. The more I can anchor a lesson to a visceral emotion – a happy one, hopefully – the more ingrained the lesson will be and the more utility it will have.

Good dog trainers know this. Bad dog trainers – or teachers or parents or bosses – will just repeat their flawed belief that 'because I said so' is good enough. It isn't. I've seen and been on the receiving end of too many lessons attempted to be taught through fear. With enough fear, you'll get the behaviour, but it'll come at a cost of collateral damage and fallout. Perhaps there will be a negative association made with the environment or a poisoning of the relationship between the teller and the doer. Perhaps the threat becomes the cue, so the subject only performs the behaviour if the threat is present and enforceable, like a circus animal. That's no way to live, and that's no way to teach.

If the options are a threat or a treat, and either will get you the behaviour, you'd be a fool not to drop your Hs. Wouldn't you, Mr Harold?

Banjo

It was 1979 and the TV wouldn't stop going on about Margaret Thatcher becoming Prime Minister. Paul Wilson on the school bus wouldn't stop going on about how Rod Stewart was allowed to say 'Do Ya Think I'm Sexy?' on *Top of the Pops*. However, it was the news that a local dog training school was going to open up at the community centre near me in Waltham Abbey that captured every sinew of my imagination. In *Great Expectations*, Charles Dickens talks about a day you've experienced that, if it were struck out of your life, would make everything completely different. This was that day.

I didn't have my own dog at the time, but I genuinely thought it perfectly fine and normal to turn up to dog training classes without one. In fact, I thought anyone who decided *not* to turn up to dog training classes, which would clearly be full of other people's dogs and therefore be epic, must be bonkers.

Old Ron was the dog trainer running the sessions and, without asking, anyone could see he was an ex-police-dog handler, purely by how he dressed in black combat trousers and boots, and the way he stood and silently watched everyone: arms folded across his puffed chest, legs far too confidently shoulder width apart.

ANOTHER DAY, ANOTHER COLLAR

I was far too shy to talk to any of the adults as they waited to go into class, but to my relief, I didn't have to. As the adults all spoke to each other, ignoring their dogs, I'd sit on the floor to talk with the dogs, ignoring the adults. Once the doors to the hall were flung open and everyone filed in, it felt like walking onto a movie set. Fluorescent lights – far too bright and no doubt unhealthy – reflected off the hard linoleum flooring, which would rat-a-tat-tat in excited Morse code as the dogs' nails bounced upon it.

The classes were very formal and regimented: 'Dogs on the left, normal pace ... forward!' Ron would command. To me, however, as I watched from the sidelines, it was like looking through a kaleidoscope. A big, bright, hairy, barking, wide-eyed kaleidoscope, and I was hooked.

I loved watching the training exercises during class, but what I loved even more was the tea break. A large hatch in one of the walls led to the community centre kitchen, where Ron's wife Sheila maintained a furiously steaming tea urn and balanced piles of Digestives onto flimsy paper plates. I'd eavesdrop intensely as owner after owner asked Ron 'my dog' questions. This is where I learned that tea breaks are when the dog trainer *really* gets to strut their stuff and drop their pearls of wisdom, as the questions asked then are the personal pinch points that owners really need help with. The group exercises were fairly generic and broad brush, whereas I've no doubt that the solutions offered by Ron during break improved the lives of dogs and owners. What an education I was getting, and all accompanied by Digestive biscuits dunked in orange squash, with a backdrop smell of disinfectant wafting from the mop and bucket in the corner labelled 'For Little Accidents'.

I loved going to Ron's dog training classes and I'd turn up religiously, either without a dog or with a dog 'borrowed' from a neighbour. Often, when I'd turn up without a dog, one of the owners would happily pass their pup to me to handle for the duration of the class.

As I grew older, I started to question the classes a little, as I began to see a few signs of stress in both the dogs and the owners. Gutted. It was like the dawning realisation that the Santa at the grotto was just a normal bloke dressed up. The lessons didn't change at all, I just started to look a little beyond the waggy tails and cuddles, and couldn't unsee the shifts in body language, facial expressions and breathing patterns as the anxiety rose. During the tea break, I realised that the owners didn't ask, 'How can I teach my dog to sit?' Instead they asked, 'How can I *make* my dog sit?'

It made me uncomfortable and it made me sad. I wanted dog trainers to remain my rock stars, wizards and saints all rolled into one. I know Ron was 100 per cent doing the best he could with what he had, and I'm forever grateful for the fire he lit under me. That said, I soon realised the ethos of a lot of the dog training I was watching was like the ethos of my lessons at school: 'because I said so'. I needed it to be different.

In addition to regularly attending Ron's classes, my love of dogs was bolstered even further during school summer holidays which always included three weeks in Ireland, with the majority of that time spent at my granny and grandad's little smallholding in Roscommon. There was no gas, no water and no toilet (not even an outdoor one – the roses in the garden were to die for) and it was the best place in the world. My grandad's dog at this time was called Buff. In later years, he also had Buff 2, followed eventually, and inevitably, by Buff 3. As with most franchises though, Buff 1 was definitely the best. He was a big, rough-coated collie and, being an 'outside dog', as many were in Ireland at the time, he wore the elements and his high mileage from working the sheep on his kind but weathered face. I'd be with Buff from sun-up to sun-down out in the cow fields. I remember those times as three weeks of baking hot weather, wearing only football shorts and wellies. With a piece of stolen Galtee cheese in my mitts, I'd spend hours teaching Buff to roll over, spin and shake hands . . . all the behaviours a grandad definitely wouldn't want their grandson to be teaching their working sheepdog! These tricks were rather beneath Buff, but he humoured me.

Ireland was fantastic in the eighties. We'd drive around the country with 'Come on Eileen' by Dexy's Midnight Runners permanently on the car radio on the way to visit various members of our huge family, all of whom lived on farms and all of whom had dogs. Like London and rats nowadays, in Ireland in the 1980s, you were never more than five metres from a dog. I certainly wasn't, anyway. It seemed every single family member on my dad's side had a

'The Original Buff'

red setter. Ninety per cent of these red setters were called Ruby. The other 10 per cent were called Ruby 2.

I was no stranger to the world of work as a child. In 1984, at the age of thirteen, I got my first Saturday job working on a stall down in Walthamstow Market, east London. The merchandise of said market stall? Stockings and tights. How's that as a character-building exercise for an anxious schoolboy? I was the Saturday boy for a lovely old Jewish fella named Ben Goldberg. Ben had been working the markets for a thousand years and he wore every day of it on his kind but cobbled face, just like Buff did back in Ireland. Most stall holders on the market were

ANOTHER DAY, ANOTHER COLLAR

Jewish, Asian or dyed-in-the-wool, leave-yer-back-door-open cockneys. The rapid-fire repartee between the players from dawn till dusk was a festival of bullshit and piss-taking in which you had to hold your own or drown. The challenge of having a laugh but still sticking my elbows out so no one took a 'bleedin' liberty' went a long way to shifting me from the anxious boy to the *mensch* you see before you today.

In wintertime, I'd be one step ahead of the weather and go to bed on Friday night wearing two pairs of pyjamas. Come Saturday morning, I'd put on my market clothes over my pyjamas in an effort to retain as much precious body heat as I could.

The two market stalls opposite Ben's stall were Ali's shirt stall and Charlie's 'Be Lucky Mum' fruit and veg stall. Ali's stall was a wall of shirts of every imaginable colour and pattern. He'd have at least a hundred shirts on display, ten across and ten up. He had a long boat hook, which he'd use to pull down a shirt from ten yards up in the air and into your trolley with the dexterity of a well-oiled ghillie. Ali's shirts were £4 each, or three for a tenner. He looked after me, though, and would let me buy one for three quid. Even today, I use the three-shirts-for-a-tenner metric to figure out if something is good value or not. If I see something advertised for £200, I ask myself: is it worth more than sixty of Ali's shirts? It rarely is.

The deal back then was that old Ben would pay me the handsome sum of £10 at the end of each day, once we'd emptied the van-load of unsold hosiery back into his lock-up. That was the official agreement, but nearly every Saturday I'd ask for my wages 'a bit early please, Ben,' so I could sprint up and down the length of the market in my twenty-minute lunch break (there were no unions for market boys!), dash into Ugly Child record shop and buy myself a Beatles or Madness album. Albums back then cost £7, which left £3 burning a hole in my pocket as I sprinted back to the stall with the vinyl clamped under my armpit, full of excitement for that precious first listen.

Once, when I sweatily flew into the shop, the assistant was playing an Elvis Presley outtake recording of 'Are You Lonesome Tonight?' I loved Elvis. In the school summer holidays, the only thing that would get me off the streets where I'd be playing with the neighbours' dogs was Mum coming to the front door to shout out that an Elvis movie was about to start on TV. On Saturday evenings, a.k.a. bath nights, I'd spend an age looking in the mirror and tapping my knuckles against my mouth, hoping for my top lip to curl up like Elvis's. It never did, Honey. This outtake recording was of Elvis corpsing with laughter as he made up silly words to the track. Rather than 'Do you gaze at your doorstep and picture me there?' he giggled 'Do you gaze at your bald head and wish you had hair?'

Hilarious.

But not so funny now, eh, Steve?

That Saturday, I spent £7 on a Madness album and 99p on the Elvis single. There would be no shirt for me that week, but as the traders' vans bottlenecked for a hopefully quick, yet inevitably slow, getaway, Charlie called me over to his fruit and veg emporium and gave me a pomegranate. A pomegranate? I'd never seen or heard of such a thing. I had zero idea what it was, let alone what it did. I sat in silence next to Ben in the van on the way back to the lock-up with the pomegranate wrapped in its brown paper bag with twisted corners on my lap, gingerly avoiding direct contact, like it was a ticking bomb. With the van unloaded, I walked back home, handed my mum the pomegranate and didn't even break my stride as I headed upstairs to listen to Suggs and the King.

I came back downstairs an hour or so later to witness my mum, my dad, my brother Anthony and my sister Maria all silently hunched around the pomegranate like it was a child in a manger. Finally, Anthony fetched the rolling pin. 'I think you're meant to hit it,' he said.

Maria shook her head. 'Someone should cut it,' she said.

All eyes turned to me. '*You* should open it, Stephen,' they said, like I was Charlie Bucket with my once-in-a-lifetime chance of a golden ticket.

The pomegranate was opened. We stared at it, bemused, like a litter of St Bernards who had just been shown a card trick. We watched it for a while but nothing happened. So we all gave up and went to listen to 'Are You Lonesome Tonight?' a good twenty times before bed.

In addition to my Saturday market job, I also used to hop off the school bus close to the town centre on Mondays,

Wednesdays and Fridays to work in the Co-Op between 5 and 8pm. I would stack shelves and *pretend* to stack shelves in equal measure. It was a joyless occupation, with not a pomegranate in sight. The only highlight was 8pm each Friday night when we were given our wages: hard cash folded into a little sealed brown envelope. Back in the day, those 'wage packets' had the corners cut off so you could count your cash without opening the envelope, like a little fingerless-gloved Fagin.

In the gloriously long school summer holidays, I would spend the first three weeks either working at other London markets in addition to Walthamstow, such as Petticoat Lane, Leather Lane or Roman Road, or out 'training' anyone's dog who would let me. My clients included Bruno, a Rottweiler owned by Mickey and Carol from two doors down, and Roxy, a toy poodle from across the road owned by Ben from the market and his wife Eileen. While most kids were making jumps for their bikes, I was forever building obstacle courses for Bruno and Roxy. I'd coax them over jumps and through hula hoops – think Metropolitan Police display dogs – for the reward of pieces of cheese and ham pilfered from the fridge back home. A third dog called Yorkie also tried to get in on the action. He lived a fair few streets away, but was always hanging around nearby. No doubt the cheese and ham had something to do with it.

ANOTHER DAY, ANOTHER COLLAR

At the age of sixteen, I made my first tentative steps into offering group dog training classes in the Waltham Cross area. A pal of mine used to maintain football pitches, and he managed to make arrangements for me to rent the land at evenings and weekends. Those training classes were bedlam. Everybody starts out being a crap dog trainer and I was no exception. I think my clients enjoyed themselves, though. At least, that was what I pinned my hopes on. I figured that if the owners and the dogs had a good time, and I could keep everyone safe, they'd keep coming back and I'd have another go at honing my skills. You can be the best trainer in the world, but if nobody's enjoying themselves you're going to be standing alone in a field. That's a scarecrow, not a dog trainer. So I made sure that my lessons were not regimented, old-school, *left-foot-forward-about-turn* affairs. And I remembered that people learn best when they're having fun.

I didn't have the money or knowledge to advertise, but my clients were incredibly encouraging. They helped me. One client designed me a poster, another sneaked it into their office and made a hundred copies, then they took 10 copies each and distributed them in their local pet shops and vets. All I wanted to do was be in a field training dogs. The enthusiasm of my clients made that possible.

Once I escaped school, the external pressure for me to get a *real* job was strong. I just wanted to be a dog trainer. However, my family, my friends and clearly everyone else I met didn't count that as a real job. 'Sure, dog training is fine as a hobby, something to do of an evening or weekend. Something to keep you out of trouble. But come on, it's just a bit of fun, isn't it? It's not a *real* job.' Even today, try finding the job title of 'dog trainer' on the drop-down box of professions when completing an online application for an insurance policy. The closest you're going to get is 'kennel maid'. *Maid?* Calm down, eighteenth century!

And so I felt I had to do what everyone expected me to do – get a 'real job'. It meant that on leaving school, I was inhaled, like so many of us were, into a job with a high street bank. The mid-eighties was a boom time for banking, so all the high street banks would open their doors at the end of summer to take in a load of school leavers. When I joined Barclays Bank in 1987, there were ten of us on the same new entrants scheme. It was crazy. Nothing seemed to be expected of us by the rest of the staff. We would clock in at 9am, hang around, do a bit of adding up, a bit of filing, mess around in what was basically the equivalent of a sixth-form common room, have lunch at the same pub every day and then bowl out again at 5pm. Life was easy but, my God, life was boring. So, so boring.

After a couple of years of mindlessly bobbing along in the real-job tide, I concluded that this malarky wasn't for me. So I gave my boss the 'thank you for the opportunities' nonsense, grabbed my standard issue 'sorry you're leaving' card, packed a pink rucksack borrowed from my pal Rob and boogied off around Australia for six months. With nothing more than a couple of vests, a pair of shorts, the obligatory shark-tooth necklace and a pair of flip-flops (referred to as thongs by the Australians – that night was a steep learning curve . . .), I mooched around Oz on Greyhound buses and had the most amazing time. Thankfully, the gift of the gab I'd learned working the markets stood me in good stead, helping me to find a lot of good people and a few bad settees to crash on as I travelled from Bondi Beach to Alice Springs.

While in Australia, I visited a pig and cattle farm, and stood glued to the dirt, mouth and eyes wide open, as I watched a kelpie (an Australian cattle dog) named Banjo work the livestock. This was the true outback – hot, hard country – where it's not only the men who are tough. So are the women, so are the livestock, and so are the dogs. Banjo was inspirational. He was like Buff on steroids. I remember watching him face off with a bull as he tried to move the herd. The bull smashed into Banjo. Banjo flew backwards and rolled through the dusty red earth a half dozen times. I can still see it now, and each time I do I feel my heart stop. I honestly thought the dog must be dead from such an impact. But nope, like a four-legged Tyson Fury rising from the canvas, Banjo bounced back up, shook himself down and, with the committed enthusiasm only a dog can have towards their work, went straight back into battle.

Banjo didn't have a back-up plan. He didn't worry about being successful or unsuccessful. He wasn't wired to think about what he'd do if he failed to move the bull.

His job was to move the bull and move the bull he would. It was quite the life lesson.

On that same farm, I remember watching a border collie working a massive drove of 200 pigs. The collie worked mostly behind the drove (look, it *is* 'drove', I've obviously googled it before going to print!), pushing them from the field towards the farmer and the barn. On one occasion, the farmer whistled the collie to 'come', but the dog's route back to the farmer was blocked by the swine. This proved to be no issue as the collie hopped onto the back of the pig at the rear of the group and ran along the backs of the other pigs in order to reach her handler. Like a rural episode of *Total Wipeout*. *Total Wipe Snout*, if you swill.

The opportunity to be around animals doing such amazing things cemented my decision to abandon 'real jobs' like high street banking and to pursue my dream of working with dogs.

Easier said than done, mate!

Home from Australia, I was still picking up whatever paying dog training gigs I could in the evenings and weekends, but it clearly wasn't going to be enough to keep the *Canis lupus* from the door. There was pressure from outside again; seeing my mates from school doing okay squeezed me away from my dream and I signed up for another 'real job'. Boy, was it a doozy. This career lasted all of forty-eight hours . . .

With no money in my pocket and a local newspaper in

my hand, I circled a curious classified job advert: 'Glove Sales Rep Needed'. I applied for no other reason than the role came with a company car and I needed some wheels to get around to my ad-hoc dog training clients in the evenings. Upon arriving for my interview, I realised that I'd gone back in time to some Gary Sparrow *Goodnight Sweetheart* set, but without the laughs. The owner of the company, I swear on my life, was called Mr Hands. He was a lovely, tweedy old chap, but so trapped in the past that he made Captain Mainwaring from *Dad's Army* look like David Bowie. I sat by his desk as he went through paper ledger after paper ledger, explaining all of the different types of glove the company provided. Who knew there were so many types of glove? More importantly, who cared? The only product of mild interest was a single chainmail glove for the butchery trade. (I did say it was only of mild interest.)

After what seemed like a decade, we stood up and he said, 'As you're going to be out on the road every day visiting clients with a box full of gloves in the car boot,' – I know, kill me now – 'you're going to need to stay in contact with us poor souls in the office. Margaret, our secretary, has something for you.' He spoke with the air of Santa asking if I'd been a good boy. *Ah*, I thought. *Superb. I'll be getting a mobile phone as a perk of the job.*

We walked along a dusty old corridor and Mr Hands rat-a-tat-tatted on a door. As we entered, he introduced me to Margaret at her typewriter. 'Margaret, this is Steve, our new sales rep. We spoke about you kitting him out so he can call in when he's out on the road?'

'Ah, yes, of course. Welcome, Steve, and if you could just sign here.'

I carefully signed a pink duplicate sheet. Margaret checked my signature, then unlocked her drawer, pulled it open and handed me ten ten-pence pieces. No mobile phone. My link to the rest of the world was a handful of change and my ability to find a working phone box.

'Just jot down each Friday how many you've spent,' Mr Hands told me, 'and Margaret will reload you.'

The interview was on a Thursday. I attempted a day's work on the Friday and I honestly cried pretty much all of Friday night. This real job might have suited some people but it just wasn't for me. I remember a creeping fear that maybe no one did a job they loved. Maybe this was as good as it gets, and then you die.

I made the most of the company car to visit dog training clients over the weekend and on the Monday, with my tail between my legs, I went into work, apologised and quit.

I continued scratching around for dog training clients, but my lack of any marketing or advertising skills meant I was soon penniless once more.

My brother Anthony is a carpenter, and a very good one at that. With the patience of a stoat and an eye for detail, even as a kid he was always happy to spend as long as it took on intricate little projects, such as making dolls' houses or little wooden carvings out in our garage,

ANOTHER DAY, ANOTHER COLLAR

between the tins of Castrol GTX, strings of onions and second-hand bikes hanging from the rafters.

I was, and still am, completely the opposite. He's all about the journey; I'm all about the destination. I honestly used to feel sorry for him when I saw that he'd been given a puzzle or some Rubik's cube rip-off as a Christmas present. I'd taunt him, 'Haha, you've just been given *work* to do, as a *present*! Your *present* is *work*!' And I'd run off to aimlessly chase a football around the street for an hour, like a chimp.

Even now, if I'm working with a dog and there's a long training road ahead of us, rather than having a huge gulf between our starting standard and our target standard, I need to create a hundred little target standards between untrained and our ultimate goal, just so I can give myself little achievable destinations. Not only will the dog get a regular supply of rewards, but I can earn regular spurts of dopamine as reinforcement for hitting mini-target 0.1, in order to then be motivated to push on to mini-target 0.2, then 0.3 and so on.

After the sales rep fiasco, Anthony could see I was getting down. 'Why don't you come in to work with me for the day tomorrow,' he offered, 'and do some labouring on site with the team?'

I figured it surely couldn't be as bad as trying to flog gloves for Mr Hands. So, the next morning, we got up seemingly two hours before we went to bed, pulled on our best dirty clothes and, in the gloom of the back of the Transit van with the other labourers, I sat in silence hugging a cement bag. The job was at Southend Airport: a big rip-out and refit of their offices and air traffic control centre. The airport itself was small in commercial terms, but it was a popular stop-off point for a lot of military aircraft. As we arrived, I saw a dozen or so bespectacled men in anoraks with cameras and binoculars standing on little stepladders pressed up against the perimeter fence in the hope of spotting a Harrier jump jet, the *USS Enterprise*, the Death Star or whatever it is these people look for. I received my instructions for the morning of my first day and eagerly got to work, keen to make a good impression in front of all of the other manly men.

My job was to rip down a load of old office walls and to carry the broken plasterboard sheets and other rubbish down four flights of stairs to load up a forty-yard skip in the car park. *Easy. I can do that.* Off to work I set.

Smash the wall.

Down the stairs.

Load the skip.

Up the stairs.

Smash the wall.

Down the stairs . . .

It was exhausting. *Surely we've got to stop for lunch soon*, I thought, but I kept quiet as I didn't want to show my desperation to the real men who were all drilling, banging and painting with intention all around me. It was almost as if they actually knew what they were supposed to be doing.

ANOTHER DAY, ANOTHER COLLAR

Smash the wall.

Down the stairs.

Load the skip.

Up the stairs . . .

Who knew lactic acid could build up in your legs just from a normal day's work?

With no sight or sound of a dinner bell, the horrible realisation dawned that these animals were clearly going to work through to the end of the day.

God, take me now!

Ah well, I thought. *At least by working through lunch we'll be finishing early.*

Smash the wall.

Down the stairs.

Load the skip.

Up the stairs . . .

Anthony eventually came over. 'Right,' he said, 'we can stop there.' Thank God! The thought of cuddling up to a cement bag in the back of the Transit van heading for home was now a warmly anticipated hot date. 'We're off down the café for breakfast,' Anthony added. 'You coming?'

Breakfast? You're kidding, right?

I asked the time.

It was only 9.30am. I honestly thought it was going-home time. And that was another 'real job' ~~crossed out~~.

Things were getting desperate.

The next advert I replied to was for a telesales role in

BANJO

London's Oxford Street. This was the final nail in the coffin of real jobs for me. I arrived at the office for my first day to be barraged by the sight and sound of a hundred or so telesales people barking down their headsets with details of never-to-be-repeated advertising space offers. The office supervisors and floor managers were all doing their best *Wolf of Wall Street* impressions, encouraging staff to stand on desks while on the phone to gain some kind of psychological advantage.

Wolf of Wall Street? Obnoxious of Oxford Street, more like.

As I sat at my desk in that awful office, I thought of Banjo the kelpie. Banjo didn't have a back-up plan. Banjo didn't worry about being successful or unsuccessful. He wasn't wired to think about what he'd do if he failed. His job was to move the bull and move the bull he would – no matter how many times he hit the dirt and had to get back up on his feet. I was finally ready to admit the truth to myself. I knew *exactly* what I was bred to do for a living. It had been – and would continue to be – ridiculous for me to do anything other than dog training.

As I walked to the tube station on my way home, I threw my tie in the bin. I'd been so sickened by my telesales experience that day that I hadn't been able to face anything for lunch. As a result, I still had my lunch money in my pocket. Outside Oxford Circus station, I handed the fiver to a homeless guy. I must have looked depressed because he said, 'What's up with you?'

ANOTHER DAY, ANOTHER COLLAR

And for some reason, I don't know why, I told him. I know, poor me, right? Telling the homeless guy *my* problems. He listened as I told him about Mr Hands, and the building site, and the awful telesales office, and my one dream: to be a dog trainer. The homeless guy was sitting on a copy of the *Evening Standard*. He ripped a page from the back, took a pencil from his pocket and scrawled something on the paper. He folded the page and told me not to read it until I was on the train home.

Bit weird, but okay. Maybe he was a wizard who knew next week's lottery numbers. We shook hands and made our farewells. As I sat on the train, I took the page from my pocket and unfolded it. There, written in beautiful calligraphy, were the following words:

I want to be a dog trainer

I deserve to be a dog trainer

I am a dog trainer

And all of a sudden, I felt like someone had taken a sledgehammer to my head.

Alfa

Having established that it's a dog trainer's life for me, by the age of twenty-one, still living at home with my parents in Waltham Abbey, I achieved my dream of owning my very own German shepherd. I'll hold my hands up now and admit that at the time I was ignorant of the plight of rescue dogs, so I went to a breeder.

Calm down, haters. I promise that the dog I'm talking about now was the first and last dog I ever bought from a breeder. I've seen a lot of good breeders and a lot of bad breeders in my time. I've also seen a lot of dogs being sold all too easily to homes that aren't appropriate, and the dog ends up in rescue. As much as I appreciate that there are a lot of good breeders dedicated to breeding healthy, happy puppies, there are still too many dogs and not enough good homes. That's why I'll always have a bias towards rescue dogs, even though of course I adore puppies. So all the other dogs I've ever lived with – over twenty and counting – have been rescue dogs.

Also, mind your own business!

Having burned the boats in order to take the island during this period, I found myself working flat out with dogs and owners to make a career of it. But despite being super busy, I still hadn't honed my business acumen, so money was a little too tight for comfort. I couldn't afford to buy a dog but I did own a beloved old Alfa Romeo car. So I had a choice: German shepherd or car? I couldn't afford both.

It was a no brainer.

The advert for my Alfa Romeo went into the classifieds and, having received a few tyre-kicking visits, I said *arrivederci* to the car and my palm was greased with the princely sum of 350 smackeroonies. What's more, I managed to keep hold of the Alfa Romeo keyring. Who's lacking business acumen now, eh? (Me, in fact: the car would be worth about twenty grand now. With or without the keyring.)

My girlfriend Gina was a friend of a friend when I first met her at a mate's birthday drinks. After five minutes, it felt like I'd known her forever. And how's this for pure kismet: Gina worked at a dog kennels and she was well and truly dedicated to making the world better for rescue dogs. Talk about it was meant to be!

Gina was the loving owner of three rescued German shepherd dogs. Zeta was the youngest. With one ear up and one ear down, Zeta had a face that permanently said quarter past eleven. Bodie was a male shepherd who was rescued from living in a burned-out Ford Escort in Epping Forest, malnourished and covered in tar. He was a real handsome boy, but good luck if you ever tried to walk him past a car with its door open. He would pull like a steam train to try to get inside the car, a place that had meant survival in his previous battle of life or death. The third

ALFA

German shepherd was the matriarchal guv'nor, Fliss. Fliss was like a poster girl for the breed-specific behaviours of a German shepherd. In layman's terms, she was a control freak. Fliss wouldn't lie down and relax at night until everyone else in the house, regardless of species, was settled. If someone got up to stretch their legs, up Fliss would get, back to work to ensure no one left or entered the flock without her first signing off on the manoeuvre.

When I was a kid, you were no one on our street unless you'd been bitten on the arse by a German shepherd. The bite was always on the backside as the dog was simply doing the job they're bred to do: trying to control the uncontrollable. But kids refuse to be in a nice tight flock and run around willy nilly. German shepherds are the army generals of the dog world, bred to feel responsible for controlling their environment. It's why we see so many issues with German shepherds announcing their frustrations at being on lead and therefore unable to corral the hectic world full of joggers, traffic and bikes.

After we pulled up outside the breeder's house in Luton, with Gina driving for obvious reasons, we headed in to see the litter, but only after I'd double-checked that we had locked all the doors, hooked one of those orange clamp things between the clutch pedal and the steering wheel and removed all valuables from the glove box. I did mention we were in Luton, didn't I? Half an hour later, with my chosen puppy cradled in my arms, we left the breeder's house and walked the twenty-five metres or so to the car.

ANOTHER DAY, ANOTHER COLLAR

It's mad, but I was now prepared to die for this little eight-week-old dog who I hadn't even met thirty minutes ago, let alone breast fed. What a powerful love dogs can draw out of us if we're open to it. Puppies are just love poultices, aren't they?

With my sparkly new puppy snug and secure on his comfort blanket in the crate in the back of Gina's car, we headed home. I was already dreaming of spending the next fifteen years sat with my German shepherd in a summer meadow, listening to the Beach Boys as we laced buttercups through each other's hair . . .

Record needle scratch

'We need petrol,' said Gina, jolting me from my fantasy as she pulled into the Esso.

'I'll get it,' I said, and walked off to pay for the fuel. Halfway towards the kiosk however, I patted my pockets and realised I'd spent every penny I had earned from the sale of my car on the pup, my new brother from another mother.

I slunk back to the car. 'What's wrong?' Gina asked.

'No money,' I said, and I pointed to the pup in the back. 'That's all of my Alfa money back there.'

'Alfa!' she said. 'That's it. That's what you'll have to call him now!'

Back home, I popped my old Alfa Romeo key fob onto his collar as a name tag and the baptism was complete. I spent the whole of that first night on the settee with him, witnessing his world record attempt to generate eight times his own bodyweight in puppy poop. It's still one of the best nights of my life.

I'm going to level with you now. I've been struggling for a good few weeks to write this chapter about Alfa. This is my fourth attempt. I think that where I went wrong with my first few drafts is that I started to write all about the adventures Alfa and I got up to: the security patrols, the competitions, the day he made me laugh out loud when he tripped but kept on walking as he looked back accusingly at the ground, like a well-rehearsed Norman Wisdom skit. The real value of our relationship, though, wasn't so much in what we did, but in how we made each other feel. (At least, I hope it was, otherwise I'll have to scrunch this draft up as well.)

Alfa magnified my emotions, my senses. He was just the most beautiful spirit. There's a series of books by Phillip Pullman called *His Dark Materials*, where each human character had their own daemon: an external manifestation of the human character's inner self. When the humans are children, their daemons shape shift between different animals. As they grow up, however, the daemon settles into whatever animal best reflects and supports their human. It turns out that my own daemon never needed to flex its shape-shifting muscles, because the animal best suited to guide me through life's trials and tribulations from the age of twenty-one was a German shepherd, and his name was Alfa.

ANOTHER DAY, ANOTHER COLLAR

'Alfa and me, a pair of pups.'

We were John and Paul, salt and vinegar, Laurel and Hardy. We were always in the same rhythm. If I'd had a bad day at work, or was down and edging towards the black dog, Alfa would quietly sit with me and breathe to the cadence of my own breath. He wasn't a 'snap out of it, life's too short, man up, let's chase cats' kind of guy. Even as a pup, he was wise enough simply to sit next to me like a seasoned old therapist, content to shelter quietly with me as we waited for the clouds to pass. And decades later, although he's gone in body, he remains with me in spirit. I can close my eyes and see his massive ears.

ALFA

I can feel the carpet of his forehead against my top lip as I kissed his head goodnight each evening. I can recall the sweet smell of his feet that he used to prod into my face as we slabbed out together on our sides in a field, mirroring each other. I can still revel in the sensation of his thick coat running through my fingers as I groomed him from shoulder to tail – a tail that always had precisely four white hairs at the very tip, like he'd ever so gently brushed up against wet paint.

As I sit here at my keyboard, it's impossible for me not to feel his breath on the back of my neck, just as I used to when he poked his head out of the dog crate in the back of my security van, placing his chin between the two headrests and onto my shoulder as we drove to a job or to our training school. That breath felt like gold dust then. It would feel even better now.

That forceful breath was not so sweet, however, as it hit my face in the small hours. I was working away from home often at this time, teaching courses all around the UK. I'd sneak Alfa into whatever budget bed and breakfast I'd found to stay in and then desperately try to sleep before having to get up at 6am the next morning for work, but Alfa would just want to be as close as possible to me. If he was in the room, he wanted to be on the bed. If he was *on* the bed, he wanted to be *in* the bed. If he was *in* the bed, he wanted to be touching me. Guess what? If he was touching me, he'd want to be under my skin. And if he was under my skin, he was wrapped around my soul.

ANOTHER DAY, ANOTHER COLLAR

Alfa was super tactile, but only on his own terms. As Kris Kristofferson would say, he was a walking contradiction. He didn't particularly like being stroked by anybody. I think he just humoured me by tolerating my proactive physical affections. However, on his terms, he loved to be touching *me*. Which was fantastic when the pair of us were chilling underneath the tree, like something from *Little House on the Prairie*. At 2am on a frosty morning in Bridgend when you're trying to get some kip, it was a bit of a nightmare.

Alfa and I had a secret tradition that no one else knew about. On the morning of Christmas Day, I would sneakily steal from the kitchen counter the disgusting little bag of giblets – neck, liver, heart and other wiring from the turkey carcass. This was in my pre-vegetarian days, when I was happier and a little less pale. Alfa and I would then tip-toe out of the house to go tracking. Tracking has always been my favourite activity to do with dogs. It involves harnessing the power of the dog's nose to follow the scent of footsteps along the ground to find treasure. Working dogs deploy this skill all the time. For military, security or police dogs, the treasure might be a fleeing criminal hunkered down in a farmhouse or up a tree. For anti-poaching dogs, the treasure might be a bad guy hidden in the *veld* of South Africa, using a drone to pinpoint the whereabouts of rhinos. For search and rescue dogs, the treasure might be a lost hiker, a missing child or a confused patient. For Alfa, on Christmas Day, the treasure was giblets. Disgusting, slimy, bloody giblets.

ALFA

'Spot the Alfa Romeo key fob'

Tracking is useful, but it's also a lot of fun. I think it's the ultimate activity because it's you and your dog going hunting together. We monkeys can only imagine the capabilities of a dog's olfactory system and, although I like to think I've taught dogs a few things to help them live in our world, when we go tracking I'm totally living in their world and that makes me such a happy camper.

ANOTHER DAY, ANOTHER COLLAR

Christmas Day meant loading Alfa into the van and driving onto any farmer's field I fancied to lay my tracks, as I knew those ruddy-faced, sausage-fingered old chaps would still be snoozing off their Christmas Eve libations. With Alfa still in the van, I would place a pole in the ground to indicate the start point, then walk up to a mile across the land, turning left or right every hundred metres or so. Along the track I would drop four or five individual pieces of 'evidence', mimicking the bad guy dropping a weapon or the lost patient losing a piece of clothing. The pieces of evidence might be an old shotgun cartridge or a small piece of cloth, something with a unique aroma distinct from the odour of the crushed vegetation created by my footsteps. At the end of the track, I'd lay the giblets on the ground. With the track laid, I would return to the van and quietly unload Alfa. I'd always wait ten minutes or so to let him clear his airways and blow out the stink of the van from his olfactory system, so when introduced to the track he would be starting with a clean palate.

We always followed a little routine before tracking. I'd put the tracking harness on him, which told him what we were about to do and helped him to get him into the zone, and I'd whisper to him, 'We're gonna to go tracking, mate. Wanna go tracking?' On catching my quiet words, Alfa would always give me that Scooby Doo 45-degree head tilt that German shepherds do so well. He'd reply with wide glassy eyes and make a high-pitched whinny from the back of his throat: 'Yeah, I wanna go tracking. Let's go tracking, Dad!'

And then we were off.

The scent that Alfa would be tracking would be generated by my previous footsteps: a heady mix of broken vegetation, scent from the soles of my boots, gases released from the disturbed soil, the diddy little microscopic beasties sadly crushed by my feet, the junky stink of my body on the air, as well as the millions of tiny flakes of skin that fall from our bodies at a constant and disgusting pace. Off we'd set, following the scent like a pair of warped Bisto kids. Nothing made me feel more alive than having Alfa ahead of me, with a 30-foot-long tracking line between us. The tracking line kept us linked but allowed Alfa to forge ahead. And I know nothing made Alfa feel more alive than having me jogging behind him along the invisible track. I always tried to put myself in his head. How was he seeing the world? How was he smelling the world? What was he hoping to find? Long shot, but I hope it's giblets!

When dogs are tracking well, they're in the flow. I like to think of 'the flow' as when the challenge syncs perfectly with the dog's peak ability. They're not thinking about their history of learning, they're channelling the history of their species. Like a great footballer or musician, they've already learned the skills like a pro, now is their opportunity to shine and perform as an artist. Alfa would correctly identify the pieces of 'evidence' I'd dropped along the way as being unusual and therefore lie behind them as a way to report his find. As we turned the final corner of the Christmas Day track, Alfa's head would rise from the ground when the scent of the treasure at the end of his mission wafted towards him. He would dig in and determinedly drive the final few steps to the end.

And as soon as he got to the giblets, what would he do?

Yep, you've guessed it.

Oh.

Actually, it turns out you haven't guessed it. Because he wouldn't devour the giblets. He'd *roll* in the stinky offal. The lunatic.

Have you ever lived with a dog that likes to roll in, say, the carcass of an old pheasant or long-dead rabbit? Something unpleasant that you'd unfortunately stumbled upon on during a walk? It normally plays out that you become suspicious all too late, as you spot your dog halt in the distance, sniff and then down they go, in slow-mo instalments, like a villain in *The Matrix* movie getting filled with lead. 'Nooooooooo . . .' you shout as you raise your arms and *Chariots-of-Fire* your way towards your dog. But it's too little too late, my friend. Already, your dog is ecstatically gyrating their spine in the rotten cadaver, like a supine Baloo.

There are a good few theories about why dogs like to roll in dead things. A common one, to which I don't personally subscribe, is that when dogs are on what might potentially be another dog's territory, they want to disguise their smell. Nah, not for me that one. My theory is pinned to the fact that dogs are super-social animals. I think that by rolling in the scent, they're gathering information from that area so they can report that data back to their social group at the den to inform the others what's out there.

Whatever the reason, Alfa would adore getting funky with the giblets and I used to adore watching him. Relax, it's Christmas! I'd unclip his harness, load us into the van and we'd sneak back into the house as the rest of the family was glued to the TV watching Noel Edmunds run up the BT Tower. Or whatever.

'Where have you been and why's the dog got red paint all over him?' my dad would ask. Happy Christmas, one and all!

Alfa had an amazing presence. But not only did he have an air of authority, he was a real beauty. Spiritually, yes, of course. But aesthetically too. I used to take him to a nearby pond to go swimming. Before I launched a ball into the water, he'd stare at me with his broad face and shiny eyes, looking like an *On the Waterfront* Marlon Brando. Once I'd thrown the ball, he'd explode into the water with a huge splash. Having retrieved it, he'd heave his saturated body out onto the bank. Did he look like a drowned rat? Not at all. He'd spit out the ball and violently shake from nose to tail. Then he'd look at me with a wet-look glance that would make Danny Zuko from *Grease* spew with envy. That dog could fall in a vat of soup and come out looking like James Dean.

As a dog trainer – and, dare I say it, hopefully a half-

ANOTHER DAY, ANOTHER COLLAR

decent one – I always try to underpin my advice with science. I want to assure my clients that I'm just not repeating some old, indoctrinated jazz that's cascaded down from my old dog trainer via my dog trainer's dog trainer, and so on. I like hang-your-hat-on-that facts, or at least advice that I can support with good, measurable evidence. If you do *this*, then *this* will happen, and this is *why* it will happen.

However, something I've always struggled to file away in a nice little pigeonhole of behavioural science is what Alfa used to do on the rare occasions when he didn't come to work with me. For example, when I'd be out doing refresher training for security dogs and handlers at venues that wouldn't permit another dog on site. Such jobs would involve visiting the security team at their place of work – building sites, nightclubs, universities – and we'd do some refresher training in situ to ensure both parties were still happy and up to scratch. Due to this aspect of my job, my hours were scattergun. Sometimes I would return home at three in the morning, sometimes midday, sometimes four in the afternoon. I had no clue what time I'd be home on any particular day until I'd thrown my bite sleeve into the back of the van along with my machismo, popped my *Pills 'n' Thrills and Bellyaches* CD into the stereo and dropped my shoulders in relief. *I* didn't know what time I was due home. Nobody *else* knew what time I was due home. The weird thing was, though, that Alfa knew. Gina could tell when to pop the kettle on because half an hour before I reversed into the driveway, Alfa would start pacing by our front door.

Now, I know what you're thinking. It was the sound of my van. It was my potent, yet somehow alluring personal smell. But no. When Alfa started pacing, I could have been thirty miles away, so unless my dog had been crossed with Steve Austin, there's no way he would have those senses. He clearly had other senses, though. Senses that are way beyond my comprehension. Dogs are phenomenal. Some days I despair at how little we actually know about them, but on those very same days, my drive to reduce that ignorance gap is what gets me out of bed in the morning.

Alfa has long departed this world, but he has never been more with me in my heart than he is now. When I took him home from the breeder that first night thirty years ago, the breeder gave me an old blanket that smelled of his mum and the rest of the litter. I used that comfort blanket to taper the old into the new. I wanted my pup to keep hold of something familiar and cherished, to support him going forward into the rest of his life.

As I write this for you now, I have Alfa's old, broad leather collar around my arm. Like the comfort blanket, Alfa's collar supports me going forward into the rest of my life. It is a constant reminder that whatever I do, no matter how simple, I should try to do it beautifully, like Alfa retrieving a ball from a pond.

It has always been about him, and it always will be.

Goat

'Do what you love and you'll never work another day in your life.'

Ah, that's nice.

They don't mention money, though, do they?

Which was really jolly annoying, as Tesco, Esso, Barclays and everyone else around me *did* mention money, and my lack thereof.

Having had my Road to Dogmascus experience with the homeless guy at Oxford Street, I was *not* going to attempt another real job. I was going to be a self-employed dog trainer.

I continued trying to build my client base. One of my clients told me about the law of reciprocation: if you give something to somebody, they're likely to feel obliged to give you something back. I'd distribute my flyers in vets' waiting rooms, but there was one particular vet who never recommended me. When I was passing one day, I decided to put the law of reciprocation into action. I went across the road and bought six Fab ice lollies, then approached the Vet's receptionist. 'You guys have been sending me loads of clients – a chocolate Labrador yesterday, a white German shepherd last week. I just wanted to say thanks very much.' And I handed over the goodies. It was all fibs, of course, but the way I saw it, the worst case scenario was that I'd have given a few nice people a few nice ice lollies. In fact, the best case scenario ensued. The very next day, they sent me a client. And now, thirty years on, they're *still* sending me clients. (Until they read this, I guess. D'oh!)

Even so, business was slow. I accepted that I didn't yet earn enough money to be doing only dog training classes, so to supplement my income I would accept any job offered, so long as it satisfied one criterion: it *must* involve dogs.

It occurred to me that at least half the adverts on TV featured a dog, so the advertising world seemed a worthwhile thread to pull on to generate some income. I wrote to as many advertising agencies as I could find in the Yellow Pages to let them know that I handled and supplied 'experienced' dog models. Some may call this blagging, however, in my defence, I never once stated what these dogs were *experienced* in. These dogs belonged to my clients, who I knew would let me borrow them. Before long, I landed my first gig through an agency for a photo shoot near Brick Lane, east London.

The gentrification of east London hadn't quite hit its straps, but there was certainly a whiff of change in the area. I turned up to the studio with a big basset hound who, as the law back then made obligatory, was called Fred. (New regulations were brought in later by DEFRA, dictating that all bassets born after 1 January 1992 be called Bertie.) Fred had kindly been lent to me for the day by one of my dog training school clients.

The shoot was for a bespoke Christmas card that

some big company wanted to send their clients. Maybe I shouldn't have, but I'd also booked myself in later the same day to do a home visit to help a couple with a newly homed puppy. It was going to be tight time-wise, but if we could get the shoot wrapped ahead of schedule, I was going to be quids in on the day.

The photographer was a lovely old pro name Ralph, who was clearly East End born and bred, and had the reassuring quietness about him of someone who knew what he was doing and didn't have to make a big dramatic fuss to justify his presence. However, also in the studio were six – *six!* – PR-type representatives of the client to oversee the shoot. You know the script: twenty-somethings in black merino turtlenecks and silly glasses, thoughtfully sucking their pen lids before interrupting each other with moot points and whataboutery. The shot was easy peasy: dog lying flat, facing camera with pair of slippers under his chin. If this wasn't in big old Fred Basset's wheelhouse, I didn't know what was. Ralph would hardly need a sports shutter. This dog was born to lie with his chin resting on a pair of slippers.

We got the shot in the first twenty minutes. Perfect. Exactly what they wanted. And exactly what I needed in order to get to my puppy home visit in time. Ten in the morning and in the can? Lovely stuff!

Ah, but the PR-types had a problem. They'd booked the studio from nine till four for a jolly nice day out of the office. They wanted to stagger back to their boss, jaded and exhausted, having dug deep but able to report that somehow, due to their creative input, the shot had eventually been managed.

I started packing up my gear. Ralph started rolling up his white background. But we both knew what was coming. We silently glanced at each other as the turtlenecks broke from their huddle around the monitor. 'That's great, guys,' one of them piped up. 'I *think* we've got it' – reader, they *had* it – 'but could we go again? And, Steve, could we get Fred to look a little more . . . poignant?'

Poignant? He's a basset, mate. Look at him. How much more poignant do you want? I don't even know how to make *myself* look more poignant!

Time ticked on. Nerves wore thin. Eventually, Ralph said he was stopping for lunch to go and grab something to eat. He asked the turtlenecks if they wanted something from the shop. 'Oh, anything really,' one of them replied. 'Maybe just some pomegranate juice and sweet chilli crisps.' Remember, Ralph was an old-school East Ender and these were the hipster invaders. He had no time for this. 'You'll have cheese and onion and a fucking Coke,' he growled. The irritation in his voice made even Fred the basset do a wide-eyed 'oh shit' double-take to camera. The turtlenecks huddled again, then broke to announce that, actually, the shot we had was great, and that they really should be getting back to the office. Hurrah! There's no school like the old school.

Another income stream I expanded to allow me to at

least remain working with dogs was the world of security dog handling. Some police dog handler friends taught me how to train security dogs, then I completed my training as an instructor of security dog handlers and soon started consulting for security companies around London and the home counties to help train their dogs and – the far trickier end of the lead – the handlers themselves.

Now, I appreciate that I'm the weird one. I know I'm a dog nut to an abnormal level. Although I shouldn't, I often catch myself getting upset if someone else who is privileged enough to work with dogs isn't as obsessive, or at least as committed, as I am. When I was on some building site as part of a K9 security unit (as they're generally known) during the freezing dead of night, I'd be out training in the dark, practising my heel work, teaching the dogs to track, trying to observe and learn just a small percentage of what they knew. I'd plan and review every single training session in my notepad and, once it was full, pop that notepad up in my loft with the rest of my training logs. I'd sleep with my dog in the back of the van during breaks and make sure they slept better, ate better and were certainly better groomed than me.

What I struggled with was that the other dog handlers weren't as into it as me. So, on individual contracts, when it got to the point where I cared more about the standard of the dogs than the actual company hiring me did, I'd knock the job on its head and walk. It got to that point often. So often, in fact, that I decided to start my own security company. That way, I could still work with dogs, but to my own obsessive standard.

I took on a few new handlers, but soon got fed up with calls from site managers at 6am to say they'd turned up on site only to see my security guard asleep at the gates. If you want a job done properly, do it yourself. So I did.

Turns out, however, that it's quite tricky to stay awake with a dog for ninety-six hours straight to guard a site all on your lonesome, which was the trick I was attempting to perform. I'd turn up on day one, bright and clean shaven, tell the site manager that I'd be doing the first shift and that we'd change handlers throughout the night every four hours, and that I'd always be there each morning for the handover. It was partly true. I *was* there every morning, but I was also there on my own every midday, afternoon, midnight and crack of dawn as well.

Gina and I married in 1999 and our son Luke was born in 2003. From that moment on, our life was turned inside out and back to front, as are all parents', and it had new meaning. Luke also adores dogs (as if he had a choice!), and has a remarkable kindness and wisdom around all animals that blows my socks off. I know in the past there were family and social occasions that I left Gina and Luke to attend without me, as I would go off to my dog training work. Well before Luke was born, but even more so once he appeared on the scene, I felt the need to work every waking hour God sent. This was a choice, not a sacrifice, and if I had my time again, I'd like to think it would be different, but I'm not sure. What I am sure of, though, is that Gina and Luke have inspired and supported me in all of my work with dogs.

I don't miss those frosty mornings and bleak nights away from my family, when the fatigue really set in. That weird, out-of-body, jetlag feeling I'd get by doing quite frankly ridiculous hours, all so I could continue to work with dogs and resist the normal nine-to-five. Come day four, I'd be seeing dots before my black-ringed eyes and would be sporting suspiciously long stubble. My justification for doing it all myself was that at least I'd be sure of not letting the client down. Although on paper I'd be earning twenty-four hours a day for four days straight, I'd be so exhausted by the time the gig was over that I'd have to sleep for three days to recover.

One such job was for a big country trade show in Middlesex, looking after all the agricultural machinery that was being exhibited in a huge field for four days and nights over a long bank holiday weekend. In addition to the machinery on display, the event also played host to the county livestock show, as well as a petting zoo for the kids. With 2am frost on the van, I was huddled inside with Alfa when, out of the dead of night, came an almighty rattling and smashing of metal from one of the paddocks behind where I was parked up.

It was on!

I grabbed Alfa's lead and my Maglite torch, and the pair of us ran over towards the bedlam. Frankly, I was bracing myself for a kicking, even though Alfa had on his 'let me at 'em, Uncle Scooby' game face.

As the torchlight settled, the baddie was exposed.

A goat.

A big, angry goat.

A big, angry goat wearing a metal five-bar gate on his head, to be precise.

Somehow, this Billy Goat Livid had got his horns stuck between the horizontal bars of the livestock gate, lifted it clean off of its hinges and was now looking for someone to blame. *Moi*. With Alfa's lead in one hand, I had to drop the torch to grab the horn of the oncoming head-banging goat. As the torch hit the ground it turned off. Yay! Leaving me stood alone in a pitch black frosty field at 2am, with a body-slamming goat fighting for his life in one hand and an 'oh my God, this is amazing' German shepherd bouncing in the other.

It got better.

As Alfa, the goat and I swayed around the field like we were performing a surreal 'Auld Lang Syne', we smashed into the housing of the petting zoo meerkats. Another win for Steve Mann K9 Security Unit Ltd. If a big prison camp security light had beamed onto us that second, it would have captured an exhausted lad who 'just wants to be a dog trainer', dancing with a goat, a German shepherd and a bunch of chattering meerkats. Like Noah on a booze cruise. At this stage, I was beginning to worry that I'd have to stand my ground until the sun came up or, worse still, until the exhibitors arrived on site. Thank goodness I eventually managed to tie Alfa up, before removing the gate from the goat's head to fit it back onto its hinges. I then wrangled the goat back into his pen and shooed the meerkats back into their housing. Simples!

As I fell to my knees, Alfa licked the mud from my face and thanked me for giving him his *best night ever*! And as dawn broke, the guv'nor of the event turned up at the gate. 'All quiet?' he said, as he pulled up to the security barrier.

'All quiet,' I said as I lifted the barrier. 'No news.'

I've never really liked the 'sharp end' of the K9 security world, but it was a necessary evil for me to get involved with back then. I felt I had to walk the walk as much as talk the talk, and it was an opportunity to be involved with dog training in another arena. As I was someone who owned a German shepherd, security was a natural groove to fall into. Although it was clearly only a stop gap for me, it forced me to learn a hell of a lot about dogs and myself. I spent so much time with dogs, day in day out, patrolling, training, sleeping in the back of the van with them, that I couldn't help but learn about what they like and don't like, like Mowgli growing up in the jungle. And by providing training for security dog handlers, I did some interesting consultancy work and got to travel around the world. One particularly fun aspect of training security dog handlers was that I insisted on visiting them at several of their sites

ANOTHER DAY, ANOTHER COLLAR

around London and the home counties between the hours of midnight and sunrise, so we could do a few real-life training drills to keep the dog focused and to progress their skillset. (And also to check that the guard wasn't sleeping!)

One such site was the Warner Brothers studio in Leavesden, Hertfordshire, where the Harry Potter movies were being filmed. Prior to my training visits, I'd often inform the handler that I would play the role of an intruder and hide somewhere on site. Their role was to search with the dog on one of their scheduled patrols, and find and 'apprehend' me. I know, butch, right? On most sites, this meant me putting on my bite sleeve, banging a few metal lock-up containers, then nestling down among the JCB diggers to await the eventual roar of 'Security officer with a dog! Come on out or I'll send in the dog!' once the dog had indicated my presence. At Leavesden Studios, however, the choice of hiding locations was much more exotic.

I remember settling down in the corner of a Harry Potter set at three o'clock one morning. Once discovered, I legged it down a few corridors with Big Dave the gasping dog handler and a rampant Rottweiler named Jesus in hot pursuit. With his hands on his knees and in between desperate gasps, Big Dave gave me my last warning: 'Security officer with a dog . . . 'kin 'ell . . . hang on . . . come on out . . . *puff, pant* . . . or I'll send the dog . . .' He released his dog and it wasn't until I'd reached the Hogwarts Express that Jesus caught up with me and got his bite. Superstar. I remember thinking at the time that there would be movie buffs all over the world willing to pay top dollar just to visit these studios, and here's me crawling all over them and playing with dogs in the dead of night. Don't tell Dumbledore!

As part of my visit, I'd often get the handler to pop their dog away so they could then run and hide for me and my own dog to do a search and find. I still smile to this day knowing that Big Dave the handler was crammed in Harry Potter's cupboard under the staircase for a good forty-five minutes while Alfa and I went and had a cup of tea and a cuddle in a warm Portacabin.

The security world had quite a few wrong 'uns in it back then, quite a few poachers turned gamekeepers, and I had to keep my wits about me, especially on the business side. Thankfully, my Walthamstow Market nous hadn't entirely left me. I was once asked by a large security company to source thirty working German shepherds for them to train to service a large London council contract for dog handlers. I knew that, over in Slovakia at the time, there were many kennels that professionally bred German shepherd dogs from strong working pedigree lines and raised them as green dogs, which meant they'd had basic training but hadn't yet learned to specialise in any particular arenas. They just loved to bite bad guys and search for tennis balls. This love of biting and balls (grow up) was sufficient for the US military to go over each September and buy sixty to eighty of their best dogs to train as their general purpose dogs (GPDs). These

ANOTHER DAY, ANOTHER COLLAR

GPDs act as sentry patrol dogs, but also double up as search dogs for explosives, bodies and contraband. So, if the US military went over in September, clever old Stevie would pop over in August and beat them to it for the pick of the litter.

After a morning of 'decoying' – wearing that big silly sleeve and running from dogs to be caught and bitten, a lot – I went back to the office of the Slovakian kennel owners to let them know which dogs interested me. I could then check each dog's portfolio folder, which contained details of the dog's pedigree, their health records, their hip X-rays and other such details. The dogs were perfect. I had a suspicion, though, that the guys selling them might not be quite so kosher. So, when I received the folder for the first dog I liked, I slyly folded the corner of the dog's X-ray prints before handing them back. 'Nice,' I said. 'Can I see the folder for dog number two?'

The guy went to the filing cabinet next door, pulled out the file of dog number two and, guess what: the corner of the X-ray presented in that folder had been folded down. They were trying to pass off the same X-ray for different dogs, the slippery sods!

Now I don't know how the US military does business, but c'mon! We're bred differently in the 'Stow! I couldn't trust these guys, so I said my *zbohoms* and made good my escape.

Too many people in this game train dogs to make money. I just wanted to make money so I could train dogs.

Max

Let me take you back to 1996. England were flying high in the UEFA football Euros, New Labour were sneaking up on the rails, the sun was shining and all this was happening against the backdrop of *Moseley Shoals* by Ocean Colour Scene. I was thankfully earning enough money to enable me to stay on track training dogs. Classes were full. There was plenty of demand for one-to-one training and the security handlers were all ticking along nicely.

Life was good. I was on the crest of a wave.

And then I got sick.

Anxiety had sneaked up on my blind side. I experienced the tinnitus nag of a voice in my ear, saying, 'Sure, you're on the crest of a wave for now, but you'll soon get found out. Nothing lasts forever and you've got away with this for long enough. Back in line, Sonny Jim.'

I found it hard to disagree with the voice in my head telling me this was all too good to be true. What right did I have to be doing a job I loved when others weren't so lucky? I decided I had to make the most of my opportunity while I still could. This resulted in me trying to work every hour God sent. I did night shifts, checking on my security dog handlers. I did one-to-one training and home visits in the morning. I did group classes in the evenings. Then I went back out for more security dog checks. Rinse and repeat. Rinse and repeat. I was travelling at a hundred miles per hour, always urging myself onto the next job before everything disappeared down the drain and I was forced to go back to Oxford Circus station to fish my tie out of the bin. I'd turned into Alice's White Rabbit. *No time to say hello, goodbye, I'm late I'm late I'm late . . .*

It was relentless and it was unsustainable. The anxiety continued to build. I stopped eating properly. I lost weight. I worried that if I didn't work twenty-four-seven, it would all disappear. I started to panic-grab every job I could. Although the quantity of my work increased, I've no doubt that the quality of my dog training classes and home visits took a downward spiral. And it was on a home visit to a lady in Chingford called Mary that I had an epiphany.

When I arrived at the house to see Mary and her ten-month-old Labrador, Max, for the first time, Mary met me at the door and before I could even kick off my shoes, she started reading from her list of all of the things she wanted to work on with her dog. She was a lovely lady who only wanted the best, but it seemed she had a sneaky little competitive edge, which rather endeared her to me.

She wanted Max to be happy.

She wanted Max to perform at his very best in dog training classes.

She wanted Max to be friendly with people.

She wanted Max to get the best out of life.

MAX

And, she admitted, she wanted to win obedience competitions with Max.

All her initial questions to me were rather specific for such an early stage in Max's training: *What were the best toys she could use to build Max's speed and improve his performance? What pitch whistle should she be using? What was the very best training vest she could buy herself?* (You know what I mean by training vest? It's a shiny polyester sleeveless jacket favoured by macho dog trainers on the continent, with loads of little pockets in the front for whistles and training tools, and two big pockets in the back for ego and insecurities.) I thought these questions were all rather premature but, as I wanted her to feel comfortable asking me any questions at any time, I nodded along and made notes as I started to form a picture of her ambitions prior to meeting the dog.

Then I met Max.

That dog was absolutely bananas.

Mad Max.

He flew into the living room, bouncing off the walls, the settee, my head. His eyes bulged like a possessed SpongeBob SquarePants. After Max had punched himself out a little, we popped him into the garden with a few nice chews to keep him entertained so Mary and I could release ourselves from our brace positions and continue our consultation.

Mary's questions had suggested she was interested in tweaking the micros, but at this stage, I was much more

ANOTHER DAY, ANOTHER COLLAR

interested in Max's macros. I asked what Max's diet was each day. I was informed that he had Cornflakes and milk in the morning, a generic supermarket kibble at lunchtime and the same at night. 'That being said,' Mary continued, 'my son Tommy works in a takeaway, so three nights a week Max joins us in a chow mein.'

Chow mein? Right.

I asked about the dog's exercise. 'Well, not much really,' she said, 'due to his age.' It turned out that poor Max would get one half-decent walk a week, but the rest of the time he was turfed out into the garden to entertain himself. There was no real exercise to get the heart pumping, blow away the cobwebs, stimulate his mind and body, or to give that sense of wellbeing and achievement after a good old blow-out around the park or fields.

'Cool!' I said, feeling less and less cool all the time. 'How about sleep?' I mentally put myself back into the brace position.

'Well!' said Mary, looking proud as she sat back in her armchair. 'We're quite clever on that one! Because he's so full of beans, I like to wake him up at 6am and then I try not to let him nap during the day, so he's nice and tired and ready to relax in the evening. My son comes home at about 11.30pm and likes to say hello and have a cuddle with Max before going off to sleep in the kitchen.' (Max that was, not Tommy. Tommy slept in a basket under Mary's bed. Maybe.)

Cool. Righto.

MAX

Mary and I (and you too, as you're reading this) now had a question to answer. We wanted to improve Max's behaviour and give him the best chance to be happy, to perform as well as he could in class and in other arenas, and to be comfortable and as friendly as possible around people. So were the keys to that lock to be found in the selection of the correct whistle, kitting the owner out in the best training vest or identifying the best toy? Or would we get a bigger bang for our buck if we improved Max's diet, sleep and exercise?

Turn your papers over now and write your answers.

Okay, everybody, pencils down.

Of course, unless we were prepared to improve Max's diet, exercise and sleep, we were never going to make decent improvements anywhere else, no matter what bloody toys we used.

Mary and I made a plan. We improved the macro, and only then did we look to improve the micro. There's no point picking out pretty tiles for your roof if the house's foundations are made of jelly.

Now, I have another question for you. Sit down, sit down! The class is over when I say so, not when the bell goes.

Are the biggest steps we can take now to improve our own lives, happiness and performance to be found in reading more books, watching more TED talks or wearing swankier clothes? Or will we make the largest gains by slightly, step by step, improving our diet, our sleep and own exercise?

ANOTHER DAY, ANOTHER COLLAR

Therein lay my epiphany.

There I was during a home visit, stating what I thought was the bleedin' obvious, when it dawned on me that I too was desperately trying to improve my performance as a professional dog trainer and be as happy as I could be in my life. However, I had arrived at this lady's door an hour earlier to share my pearls of wisdom having just slept in the back of my van for two hours with Alfa, having worked through the night – a night that had me flying all around London with time only for a couple of mouthfuls of Pot Noodle at the traffic lights.

As I left Mary's, I realised it was time for me to walk the walk and not just talk the talk. I pledged to myself that I would make some little tweaks to tidy up my sleep patterns, my diet and my exercise regime. Maybe you could also make the same pledge? Take small steps. I'll admit my first step at the time to improve my sleep wasn't a commitment to get a solid eight hours each night. No, my first baby step was to have my own pillow in the back of the van! Small *achievable* steps. Then the next step, then the next.

I hope that consultation went some way towards improving the lives of Mary and Max. But I know beyond doubt that, thanks to Mary revealing the questions that needed answering, my life certainly improved from that point on.

Health is wealth, baby!

MAX

The story of Mary and Max reminds me of another dog training home visit I did around the same period in Bethnal Green.

The lady, Joan, was a stuff-and-nonsense, Lambert-and-Butler-toking pensioner from the East End. She had a pair of beautiful jet-black male entire (not castrated) Staffordshire bull terriers. Their names were Ronnie and Reggie, obvs. These two dogs were super friendly but had pent-up steam coming out of their ears, like a frustrated Oliver Hardy seconds prior to his bowler hat firing off from the top of his head.

I started with my standard opening gambit: 'What do the dogs eat?'

Without drawing breath or taking the fag from her mouth, Joan said, 'Well, first thing in the morning we always have a coffee each...'

Now, as much as I pride myself on my show-no-judgement poker face during consultations, the mask clearly fell at this revelation. Seeing me wince, she leaned forwards across the table, put her face inches from mine, took the cigarette from her mouth and whispered menacingly, 'They don't have sugar, you know?'

'Fab!' I said, giving her a terrified grin and pretending to draw a massive tick on my notepad. 'Next question...'

Woofy

Anxiety is a heavy weight to carry around in your gut, isn't it? At least fear has the courtesy to justify the cortisol seeping into your bloodstream. With fear, you're faced with the scary thing. It has an evolutionary function. It drives you to *do* something about it, to put distance between you and the threat. Once the scary stimulus is no longer present, the fear subsides. Fair enough. It's an honest deal. Fear does exactly what it's paid to do.

Anxiety, however, is a snide guest that always outstays its welcome. It is the fear of fear, the fear of an unknowable future. The fear that something bad *might* happen.

Well of course something bad *might* happen. Anything *might* happen. But I'd rather not have the hollow legs and darting eyes to remind me, thank you very much.

Anxiety can be bloody debilitating, and I should know. I was a normal, happy-go-lucky kid straight out of the packet, with normal, happy-go-lucky factory settings. However, my first day at infant school, aged five, changed all that. I was packed off to St John Fisher school in Loughton. The first time being away from home from 7.30am to 4.30pm is a million years on a five-year-old's timescale. I was away from my dog pals in the street. I was away from my football. It was just a stretch too far of the umbilical cord for me at the time. On the rattly

ANOTHER DAY, ANOTHER COLLAR

old double-decker school bus that stank of dust, I sat in silence, staring out the window, tilting my head backwards and widening my eyes so the tears wouldn't run down my cheeks in front of the other kids. They all seemed to know each other. They didn't really, of course, but that's how it feels when you're anxious.

The die was cast in the first hour by the headmistress, a nun called Sister Austin. During the register, she 'hilariously' called me the Mann-Boy in front of the rest of the class. Hardly a gag to warrant a Netflix special, but back in 1975 it was enough to bring the house down. From that very moment, I started to count down the days until I could leave school and spend all my time with dogs. I ached to be back home, making hula-hoop jumps for Bruno and Roxy. I vividly remember the rest of that first day in class. I crossed my arms on the desk and placed my forehead on my forearms, face down to the flip-top desk, so the other kids couldn't see me crying. I can smell the scent of the old wooden desk lid. I can feel the pencil marks swelling into my face as my hot breath and salt tears reactivated the dormant snot and tears of the kids who had cried before me.

Here's the cost of that comment from Sister Austin: from that day, aged five, through to the age of sixteen when I left school, I vomited every single school day morning. Saturdays, Sundays and school holidays? All clear, no problem. Monday to Friday term time? Alarm, bathroom, vomit, *Popeye* on *TV-am*, head out to wait for the school bus with the other kids for another day of avoidance.

Anxiety. It wasn't going to go away. But it wasn't going to beat me either. It was going to create protective scar tissue for me. Even now – and I'm wary of sharing this – if I'm filming, speaking at a conference or presenting a course for the first time or to a new audience, you can guarantee two things: one, I'm going to try my absolute best, and two, I'm going to be sick before the event.

Feel the fear and do it anyway? Nah, that's amateur stuff.

Feel the *anxiety* and do it anyway? Now that's for the rock stars.

Perversely, a lifetime of hair-trigger anxiety has given me a lot of confidence to help others. It's given me a welcome perspective, a degree of empathy and a toolkit for supporting anxious dogs, anxious owners or anxious students on my courses. I can spot from a mile away in either species the tight mouth, the hard eyes, the tucked tummy or the roached back. I notice the dog pretending to discover a new sniff, or the student exaggerating the importance of their decision to choose a blue pen or a black one, and identify these as coping strategies, displacement behaviours as a diversion from their anxiety.

This is why, for as long as I live, I'll never stop saying to anyone who will listen: how a dog *feels* is far more important than what a dog *does*.

For too long, dogs have been measured first and foremost for their obedience: sit, down, come. If you look at a new owner with their new puppy, they'll often practise 'sit' a thousand times before they concentrate on anything else.

ANOTHER DAY, ANOTHER COLLAR

But any behaviours taught in the safety and security of the puppy's new home will go right out of the window if the dog hasn't had the opportunity and support to feel robust, resilient, confident and optimistic, to build up an immunity to the outside world and what it can throw at them.

It's the same when I'm lecturing or presenting to dog trainers and behaviourists. I'm never going to start the lessons with smarty-pants learning theories and digging into the minutia of behavioural studies if I haven't first chatted and relaxed with the students. I want them to talk to me as much as possible, to allow them every opportunity to breathe, soften their spines, tilt their head and smile, to realise I'm not another Sister Austin. Only when I see their shoulders drop, their jaws relax and that they stop fiddling with their pencil cases do I start dropping the knowledge bombs.

If the student or the dog is anxious on the inside, then on the outside they may look disobedient or uninterested. It's not that they're choosing not to learn, it's that they *cannot* learn. In fact, scratch that: they *are* learning, it's just that they're not learning what you think you're teaching. If they're anxious, they're learning that they don't feel comfortable or happy in your presence. They're learning that 'lessons' and 'classes' don't make them feel good, that they're something best avoided.

Puppy classes, staff meetings, dates, job interviews, school classrooms . . . it's all the same.

It's absolutely ludicrous and frankly embarrassing to see

dog trainers out there on social media, harping on about how to 'correct' – AKA punish – a dog for disobeying their owner. There are multiple products on sale, such as remote shock collars, designed for the sole purpose of agitating or scaring your dog into coming back to you when called. To hell with that. Using such punishment in dog training creates an ethos of 'something bad *might* happen'. An ethos of anxiety. An ethos of 'because I say so'. That's not teaching. That's threatening.

My teaching demands positive reinforcement front and centre. 'Hey, here's an opportunity to get something *awesome* if you do behaviour X.' Repeat behaviour X enough times and eventually the behaviour itself feels great because it's associated with something awesome. Not only that, but the owner has now also been repeatedly associated with something awesome, making them, in the eyes of their dog, also *awesome*.

How do you want your dog to feel when training with you? Under threat or full of optimism? Which method will increase enthusiasm and joy? If the student feels good when learning, lessons are easy. How the student *feels* will always take priority over what the student *does*.

If your dog trainer tells you how to discipline your dog, how to punish your dog or how to correct your dog, get a new dog trainer. Don't be anxious of your dog trainer and don't allow your dog to become anxious of you.

Woofy was an anxious dog. If you observed her body language, she'd tick all the boxes.

Woofy was a pretty, medium-sized tan cross breed with a white chest and black eyeliner. She had been rescued from the streets of Romania and rehomed to a family in the UK in 2001. As soon as Woofy's owners unloaded her from the back of their car at my training field, she stood absolutely still, mouth shut, lips pursed tightly forward. The base of her ears slunk back. She had tension in her neck. The whites of the eyes, known as sclera, were glaringly visible. Her hips were rock hard and coiled, causing the spine to be roached and the tail to be tucked, covering her genitalia in the hope of leaving no trace of her existence to others in the location. *Another day of avoidance.* We, us humans, store tension in our neck and shoulders, dogs store a huge amount in their back end.

It would have been bananas to start 'teaching' exercises like 'sit' and 'down' to Woofy at this point. If we had attempted to teach her exercises at this stage and inadvertently added too much pressure, then not only would we have poisoned the training field, me and the owners, but also the very idea of her getting out of the car. So much could go wrong. Instead, we humans just sat on the grass and hung out, with Woofy on a nice long lead of five metres or so. The owners kept the lead relaxed and slack, so Woofy never felt restrained or cornered. They let her quietly take in the environment, first with her eyes and then, when she was ready, with her nose, as she dropped her head to continue her fact-finding mission. Nothing was asked of Woofy, but here was the first win. She felt relaxed enough to stop scanning the horizon with her eyes for baddies, then to drop her head and her guard and have a good sniff. So much more important than a 'sit' or a 'down'.

I asked the owners to say nothing to their dog (which is the hardest command I ever issue in dog training). Instead, I wanted them to watch Woofy, observe her body language and understand how she was feeling, so in future they could respond accordingly. Communication doesn't start when someone speaks. It starts when someone listens. After ten minutes, Woofy's mouth relaxed, her jaw dropped to reveal her bottom teeth and her breathing became more regular and rhythmic. This allowed her rib cage to lose some of its tension, opening up her hips and allowing her tail to adopt a more neutral position. You can keep your televised Crufts heel-work competitions; this is where the action is.

A few minutes later, and with no prompting, Woofy looked to her family and, when she did, they offered a treat. Woofy walked over but didn't take the treat. No worries. Rehabilitation is a process, not an event. I asked the owners to pop the treat away and to allow Woofy to be quietly next to them. A few minutes later, Woofy exhaled and lay down next to her owners. Amazing!

A few long gentle strokes along Woofy's back, shoulders to hips, and we were done. We popped her back into the car and the owners also finally exhaled. Delighted that Woofy had chosen to lie next to them, and with a newfound appreciation that the quickest way to teach a dog is slowly, we unloaded Woofy from the car again and repeated as before. Now her scanning took less time and she was quicker to check in with her family. She was also trusting enough to take the treat. Be still my beating heart. I live for this stuff.

The family's homework was to do this twice a day for the next ten days, starting in a familiar location. Only when Woofy left the car and immediately looked to the family with relaxed body language were they then to go to a new location for their next session.

Helping Woofy wasn't about teaching any specific 'dog training' exercises. It required a holistic approach to deal with her anxiety and let her know she was safe and that she had the agency to choose whether to stick, withdraw or go on to the next level in each environment. She spoke through her body language and her family, who loved her, listened.

One of my favourite series of training sessions took place a couple of years later in 2003, when I was called in by a family to help their son Sean learn to cope with the anxiety he had around dogs.

Little Sean was a sweet ten-year-old boy who had started to avoid going outside because he'd had a bad experience with a dog jumping up at him when playing in a football match for his local team at the park. To support him, and with every good intention, his mum had tried to help Sean 'get straight back on the horse', but then they had another incident with a dog. It was nothing too drastic, but it was enough for Sean's trust in the outside world and, sadly, of his mum, to deteriorate. Sean's immediate fear had malignantly cascaded down into longer term anxiety and it had stopped him doing the one thing he truly loved: practising football, so that one day he could play for a top team.

Fear is fear. Anxiety is anxiety. Mammalian body language is mammalian body language. I knew enough about my own anxious body language as a kid and, as you know, I dig dogs. I was well positioned to help.

Sean's bedroom had the usual posters of footballers on the wall. Mostly Arsenal, which was another reason to like him and a nice piece of common ground to help us break the ice. We chatted together to come up with a plan. Sean really wanted to be able to go to the park again to play football with his mates. He really wanted to be okay. He didn't *want* to be anxious. So I promised him that we'd work together until he was cool around dogs. I told him that when we trained together, the most important thing was how he felt, not how close he got to dogs. If at any stage he felt uncomfortable, or if he wanted to walk away, then all he had to do was tell me. If he didn't want to say it out loud, he just had to squeeze my hand and we'd retreat together from whatever was bothering him.

ANOTHER DAY, ANOTHER COLLAR

With all my students, both two legged and four, choice and agency always provide the power steering. I know that if my students are aware they can hit reverse at any time, they're going to be more confident and bolder going forwards. Control is empowering. I needed Sean to feel in control of his environment.

I suggested that we go outside into the cul-de-sac where he lived, just to hang out together, maybe kick a football around. I wanted him to do something he was familiar with and good at. Standing still doesn't help anxiety at all. Just look at all the people waiting for an interview or an important phone call. They're pacing for a reason.

Of course, to help Sean, I was going to need a dog, and who better for the gig than Woofy? Her family were more than happy for me to borrow her for the session, so she could help Sean the way Woofy's family had helped her. I said to Sean that, once he was comfortable outside, and if he was happy to let me, I was going to ask my colleague to unload the beautiful Woofy from the van, which would be parked fifty metres away down the road. I explained that Woofy would be on the lead and I told him a little about her: what she looked like, where she came from, who she lived with and how gentle she was. I told Sean that Woofy used to be quite like him, that when she first came over from Romania, she was a little anxious around people. But not now. Now she was happy, calm, relaxed and lovely. I suggested that we do the same kind of lessons I did with Woofy that had helped her with her anxiety, although I told Sean that, when *he* got it right, I wasn't going to rub his belly or ask him to chase a tennis ball for me. 'Deal?' I asked.

Sean laughed. 'Deal,' he said.

I noticed while we were chatting that each time Sean or I mentioned the word 'dog', he would rub his belly a little. It made sense to me because that's where the anxiety venom lies in wait. I tested it a few times as I spoke. I would talk about football: no tummy-rub. I would talk about other animals: no tummy-rub. But when I spoke about dogs, Sean would rub his tummy. 'Okay, Sean,' I said. 'We're going to have a tummy score. When we're outside, you're going to tell me how you feel in your tummy. A score of one out of ten means you feel absolutely fine. A score of five means you're not completely happy. A score any higher than five means we're going to head back towards your house.'

To check his understanding before we left the house, I said, 'Imagine if we turned on your TV now and saw that Arsenal were beating Tottenham five–nil. What would your tummy score be?'

'Zero!' Sean grinned.

'Cool, me too. Let's say we went out the front door and a monkey jumped on top of a dustbin and made a loud noise next to us. What do you think your tummy score would be?'

'Four, maybe?'

Made sense.

'How about, and here's the big one, you're sat in your

bedroom quietly, then all of a sudden, a fierce dragon smashes through the door breathing fire and jumps on the bed next to you. What's your tummy score now?'

'One,' said Sean.

'One? How come?'

'I love dragons!'

Fair do's. Clearly fear and anxiety are in the eye of the beholder.

'How about if a puppy came in?' I said.

Sean looked to the floor as his hand drifted towards his tummy. 'Nine,' he said.

We headed outside into the quiet cul-de-sac and kicked a football. After a little while, I asked Sean for his permission to ask my friend to take Woofy from the van, on the lead, fifty metres from us. Sean took my hand as we watched Woofy get unloaded.

'What's your score Sean?'

'Two.'

'Good boy. That makes sense. Let's hang around here for a while, see what happens to your tummy.'

We waited. We chatted. Eventually, Sean's eyes shifted from Woofy back to me as his hand dropped from his belly. 'What's your tummy score now?'

'Zero,' he said.

'Zero already? Wow! Shall we go forwards a bit?'

'Okay, but not too far.'

'You tell me how many steps.'

'Let's do twenty,' said Sean.

'Tell you what, let's do ten first and then see how we feel.'

Ten steps closer to Woofy, we hung out for a bit. 'Tummy score?' I said.

'Three.'

'Nice one, mate, you're being quite brave here, you know. Let's hang out. If at any point you want to go backwards, you just squeeze my hand to tell me and we'll head back. But I reckon if we wait here long enough, that tummy score might go a little bit lower. Let's just wait and see.'

We waited and we saw: the tummy score drifted back down to zero.

We carried on along this path of desensitisation for another couple of sessions, with Sean dictating the pace and always having the casting vote on whether to go forwards, stick or reverse. By the third session, Sean was stroking, feeding and walking Woofy on a lead, with me passively walking alongside them. That was Sean, Woofy and the cul-de-sac sorted, but we had to proof Sean's resilience by practising in as many different locations with as many different dogs as possible. No problem – I had access to lots of different dogs and the world is full of locations.

The final big shift was to substitute me out of the game and pull Mum off the bench to join Sean's team. Soon, Sean was happily and independently heading back over to the park on a daily basis to play football with his pals. A few weeks later, Sean and his mum called to tell me how well he was doing around dogs, and to let me know that thanks to all his football practice at the park, he'd been spotted by a scout and invited to go for a trial with – you guessed it – Tottenham!

'Chin up,' I told him. 'We all have to start somewhere, but if in ten years' time you score against Arsenal, you'll be in trouble . . .'

With an emphasis on choice for the learner, we can all be brave enough to allow our abilities to blossom. There's no need for embarrassment, humiliation, bullying or forcing.

There's no need for punishment.

There's no need for anxiety.

Itzy

Not all tension is equal.

From my experiences with anxiety, and my realisation that it wasn't going to stop cropping up, I decided to meet the bugger head on. I continued to explore anxiety and the tension it triggered, both in myself and in dogs.

Tension is everywhere. You'll probably experience it in most of the activities you actually enjoy doing.

Movies? All good films bring you to a cliff edge, dangle you there for a bit of the old suspense and give you a big payoff as the tension is released with a happy ever after.

Dog-to-dog play? Look at them both as they run, run, run and then *freeze*. They build tension, then boom, they're off again. They appreciate that with no tension, there can be no release.

Sport? A good game is never ten–nil. A good game is five–four or two–two. A good match is never a walk-over. It has to have tension.

Comedy? Build a topic, make it awkward, hold the silence, then enjoy the release and relief facilitated by the laugh.

Music? Think or your favourite tune. I bet the verse builds to a point, holds, then resolves into a satisfying chorus.

ANOTHER DAY, ANOTHER COLLAR

Teaching? Create a puzzle and build tension so the student seeks the release only the discovery of a correct answer can give.

Anxiety's a nasty little scumbag, but tension is all right. It can be valuable. It's a bit like stress. Too much is unhealthy, but a little here and there is important to get things done.

As I've grown older and battled my own demons, I've realised that anxiety and tension are beyond my control. But what is completely *in* my control is my response to them. If I back away from something on the horizon causing tension, all I'm doing is stretching the elastic band, creating even more tension. I've realised that tension only happens *before* an event. It never happens during it. Boxers are tense before the fight, not in the ring. I can deal with anything when I'm in the moment because I have to.

I've learned that facing forwards and just 'doing' is the key to releasing anxiety and tension, to the extent that I take on all challenges before tension and anxiety have even had their first coffee of the morning. That feeling of release is so good that I've found it addictive. I go looking for it. I even invent my own new challenges so I can get that dopamine kick of finding the release. That buzz of release from tension can be addictive.

We had a beautiful little sable German shepherd, named Itzy because of her size. Itzy used to get a kick out of chasing and creating tension, just so she could get the rush of release. She'd be in the living room with a tennis ball

ITZY

in her mouth, which she'd drop and deliberately knock under the sofa. She'd then spend the next five minutes with a hard body, barking and pushing her front leg under the furniture to try to swipe the ball out. And *pow!* As soon as the ball tried to make its escape, Itzy would pounce like a puma to grab it. With a soft body facilitated by the release and a job well done, she'd trot around the room parading her trophy. A couple of minutes later, she'd drop the ball, whack it under the sofa, create the tension and go to work again to get her fix.

Itzy, like many dogs, enjoyed a few laps of the zoomies with a pal, be it another dog or a human compadre. We'd be walking along in a field or in our garden, when all of a sudden, she'd face me, crouch, freeze, tense up her body and beg for release. I'd look to her, wait a few seconds to build the tension and then, like Spiderman landing on a skyscraper, I'd strike a pose and freeze myself. This gave Itzy the green light to bomb around at a hundred miles an hour, in no particular direction but cross-eyed with the joy of successfully finding another release. Even though three years earlier Max had held a huge mirror up to me to illustrate the important things in life, let's just stay I was still somewhat of a work in progress. Learning is a process, not an event, remember?!

Some people around me framed my constant search for tension and release as a tad unhealthy, labelling me a 'workaholic'. I certainly didn't see it that way at the time. For starters, it never felt like work. It gave me a buzz and it served to beat anxiety and tension at their own game. By the time I reached my mid-twenties, however, it was safe to say that my drive was at an unhealthy peak, as I constantly looked for or created my own tensions so I could ride the high of the release. If I wasn't out training dogs and running classes, I'd be out searching for or trying to execute contracts far too large for a one-man-band like myself at the time. The buzz from biting off more than I could chew, and successfully chewing it, was too much to resist. I was constantly throwing tennis balls under the sofa to prove (to whom, I'm not sure) that I could get them myself. I was the most boring person in the world to be around, unless, of course, you were a dog or an accountant.

In my desperation to make a go of it, I'd work every hour possible. I'd often miss birthdays, parties and other important social events. Don't get me wrong, I'm absolutely not playing the world's smallest violin here. I'm not pretending these were *sacrifices* I made to give my family a better life – they were choices. To call them sacrifices would be a sneaky way of trying to paint myself as less selfish than I actually was at the time. I *chose* to work with dogs and search for new challenges above everything else because there was nothing more I'd rather do. I was desperate to get as much done as possible before the spectre of getting found out became a reality, and I'd have to slot back in line and get a real job.

If it wasn't bad enough for my family that I thought

about my dog training business every waking moment, my obsession got to the point where I would startle the household awake by shouting out dog training lessons in my sleep at 2am. It was clear something had to change. We had a summit meeting.

'This is bonkers,' Gina told me. 'All you do is think about dogs! I need you to promise me that you'll do at least one thing per week that isn't dog related. Something that's completely separate so you can concentrate on yourself, to stop your bloody mind racing about dogs.'

I agreed. I researched things I might do to concentrate on myself and decided on yoga. So, with my yoga mat tucked under arm like Sid James heading to the beach, I bowled off to my first yoga class.

I was looking forward to the class, as I appreciate any opportunity to consider teaching from the student's perspective. I'm always looking for ways to improve the way I can teach dogs and owners. Over the years, I've had lessons in guitar, piano, golf and languages. I haven't so much attended the lessons for the subject matter itself, but for a chance to discover teaching techniques to adopt – or to definitely avoid. I love teachers who not only tell you what and how to do something, but, most importantly, tell you why. I honestly believe that if a student, owner or dog understands the why, they'll put the lesson to good use and apply the necessary effort. If they don't understand the benefit, they won't commit.

As well as the usual sharing of knowledge, I like to

ANOTHER DAY, ANOTHER COLLAR

consider the physicality of how the teacher tries to present their lesson. When I was younger, I used to practise my presenting skills in front of a group of dogs, treating them as if they were humans attending my class or seminar. My challenge was to see if I could keep the dogs engaged and focused on me solely with my body language, then solely with my tone.

I've never been one for physically taking someone else's dog off them in class to perform and demonstrate a particular exercise. To me, that's setting the dog or the owner up for a fail. If I perform the demo, there's a good chance the dog will behave perfectly for me – and I should bleedin' well hope so because this is my job. It's all I think about. If I then hand the dog back to the owner – who is not a freak like me, but a normal person with a normal life – they of course won't have the same skill set. The result is often the owner thinking: *If you do if for Steve, why won't you do it for me?* Therein lies a recipe for a relationship breakdown. It's far better that I stay at arm's length and coach the owner to coach the dog.

Once, I went up to Denmark Street in London to buy a guitar. I knew exactly the model I wanted and had the money ready to go. I entered the shop, pointed to the guitar on the wall and said to the assistant, 'Can I see that one, please?' The assistant pulled the guitar down off the wall and started playing it himself. He was brilliant, doing so much more with the guitar than I could ever do. When he finally got off his knees to collect the roses thrown to him by the admiring onlookers, he offered me the guitar and said, 'There you go, mate.'

No, thanks! He had completely poisoned the guitar for me. There was no way I was going to attempt my ham-fisted 'London's Burning' following his 'Stairway to Heaven . . . and Back'. He should have pulled down the guitar, handed it to me and said, 'There you go. Do you know a G chord? Give that a go. Sounds good, doesn't it?' It would have been a done deal. He'd have got his cash and I'd have walked out of the shop still thinking I was going to be the next Jimi Hendrix.

I particularly liked my yoga teacher Veronika because not only did she explain what she wanted us to do, but *why* she wanted us to do it. At the beginning of the class, when she wanted to engage everybody and get the room revved up a little, she would ask us all to breathe in for five seconds then out for four seconds, then in for six seconds and out for four seconds, then in for seven seconds then out for four seconds. She explained that by emphasising our in-breaths at the beginning of class, we were engaging our sympathetic nervous system, the part of the nervous system dedicated to higher activity, such as fight or flight.

At the end of the class, when she wanted everybody to come down a little and relax, she asked us to breathe in for two seconds then out for four seconds, in for two seconds then out for six, in for two seconds and out for eight. By extending the exhalation, she explained that she was

ANOTHER DAY, ANOTHER COLLAR

getting us to engage our parasympathetic nervous system, putting the vagus nerve to work to help us relax. Less fight or flight, more rest and digest. (To be honest, I shouldn't really be sharing this information with you because, as Veronika made us promise, 'What happens in vagus . . .' Sorry, I can't even finish that. Apologies.)

I was at yoga classes to distract me from dog training, but, of course, *my mind drifted*. . .

When I'm working with a dog struggling with anxiety or arousal – be it tension around other dogs, wariness of humans or whatever the trigger may be – I often see that the dog will have their mouth closed when under too much pressure. That initial inhalation then holding of the breath shows that they are riding the clutch at an amber light, poised for fight or flight. To reassure myself that a dog is relaxed and happy during training, I look for a nice open, soft mouth. It tells me that the face is free from tension, that the breathing is smooth and open, and the dog is happy in the presence of whatever stimulus we're working with.

We do the same thing. Imagine you're home alone one night, it's midnight and you're about to go to bed. As you turn off the lights, you suddenly hear creepy footsteps upstairs. You'll inhale deeply and hold your breath. This allows you to hear better of course, but importantly, it also engages the old fight-or-flight instinct. But then you think, *Ah, it's only the cat. LOL*, as you open your mouth to let out a big sighing breath of relief, allowing you to relax and drop your hunched shoulders. (*But wait*, you think. *I don't have a cat!* You widen your eyes, pick up the rolling pin, inhale deeply again and tighten your mouth . . . [*Fade to black, roll credits* . . .])

I was going to yoga to forget about dog training, but all that was happening was I was thinking about dog training at yoga.

Amber

Recently, I've spent a good few hours in my loft, going through my old dog training logs and diaries as a memory-jogging exercise for the content of this book. I'm not one for keeping mementos and trinkets normally, but my old training logs are precious to me.

For over thirty years, I've made notes of every single dog training class and one-to-one I've done. Want to find out the wind direction of the first tracking session I did with Paul and Zeus on the morning of Tuesday 4 March 1997? Or perhaps the mealtimes of Billy the barking golden retriever, who I visited Sunday 6 June 1999? Or the details of the vet's follow-up report for Finn the Jack Russell, who bit his owner whenever they tried to attach the lead to his collar twenty-one years ago? No problem. (South-west to north-east; 7am and 5pm; an ear infection – so no wonder poor Finn was suspicious of hands coming towards his head.)

One such training log I came across was from a home visit I did in 2003 to a lady named Sally, who lived near London Bridge. Sally was a dentist. Her profession has no relevance to this story at all, but here it is, written in my training log of Tuesday 1 July. A week previously, she had taken on a King Charles cavalier from a friend and was determined to get it right. As the door to the apartment opened, I was greeted by a determined-looking Sally, who proceeded to read from a long list of what she wanted me to train her new dog, Amber, to do. 'I want her to walk nicely on the lead, come back when called, understand "sit" and "down", give paw, go to her bed, not go on the furniture, not jump at visitors, be good with other dogs, be happy in the car . . .'

Go-getter Sally had only adopted the dog five days ago!

This is not an unusual occurrence, and to be fair, the owner generally just wants what's best for them and their dog. So when faced with a long list of 'wants', I've learned to not scream, 'Time out!' Instead, I join the owner on their own rhythm and ask, 'And what else?' each time they draw breath. When they've eventually punched themselves out and exhausted their specialist subject of 101 things to teach a dog, I put my pen down, suck a thoughtful tooth and say, 'Great. Lots to be getting on with then! Fifteen exercises to teach? Wow! I wonder, though, if there's *one* exercise that could make the other exercises easier?'

Spoiler alert: eye contact. It's always eye contact. If the dog happily and optimistically learns to make eye contact with their owner, it makes everything else easier, or even redundant. If the dog's eyes are on the owner, chances are so are their ears. If the dog is ready and open and listening, the owner only has to ask once. If the dog's eyes *aren't* on the owner, forget about it! If the dog regularly offers eye contact while walking on the lead then, hey presto, we have loose-lead walking. Teaching loose-lead walking as an

AMBER

additional and separate exercise is now redundant. If the dog is regularly checking in with the owner during off-lead walks, then teaching 'Come' has just become much easier. And so on.

I explained to Sally that the US military has a mantra when trapped in an ambush situation with far too many problems to address at once: prioritise and execute. One layer at a time. To prioritise Sally's admittedly lower stakes but nevertheless mammoth wish list, I left her with a revised to-do list:

1) Teach Amber eye contact
2) Play with Amber

That was it. Just two exercises. Every day for two weeks.

Once Amber had learned that 1) looking at Sally allowed access to the keys to the kingdom, and 2) Sally is fun to hang around with, everything else became much easier, or redundant. It's better to go fifteen metres in one direction than one metre in fifteen directions.

If you're wondering how to teach eye contact, here are the highlights:

- Grab a handful of treats in your fist and face your dog.
- Hold your treat-laden hand out to the side of your dog's face.
- Say nothing!
- Let your dog sniff, lick and stare at your hand. Wait patiently.

ANOTHER DAY, ANOTHER COLLAR

- When your dog looks at you, say 'Good!', open your hand and let your dog snaffle a treat.
- With repetition, your dog will look to you sooner and sooner. Make sure your say 'Good!' and treat each time.
- Practise this in as many different places as possible.

The above is the *formal* training. The *informal* route, to run alongside the formal route, is for you not to ask but to wait for eye contact from your dog, prior to them accessing something they fancy. For instance, after dinner, when they want to run from the kitchen to the garden for a play, don't just open the door. Wait with your hand ready on the door handle as your dog looks out to the beckoning birds and squirrels. When your pup looks up to you, say 'Good!' and open the door to reinforce the behaviour of eye contact.

Any questions? No? Good!

As I flicked through Sally and Amber's notes, my mind naturally drifted towards Tupperware. I'm sure that you, like me and like any other sane person living in civilised society, have a love/hate relationship with plastic storage containers. Up until a couple of weeks ago, in our house, we had every size, shape and colour of container you could imagine. In addition, we also had every size, shape and colour of lid you could imagine. However – and here's the kicker – it seemed that we never had the right lid to fit the right container. In an attempt to rectify this situation

AMBER

– and you'll recognise this move – we bought even *more* plastic containers and crammed them into the bulging Tupperware cupboard, so we would at least have *some* matching sets. This conversely made it even harder to find matching sets when the cupboard was opened and the T-ware came a-tumblin'.

I call this the Tupperware Paradox. The more containers you have, the harder it is to find a matching lid. When I first started teaching dog training classes, I was so desperate to impress that, in an attempt to convince people I knew what I was talking about, I tried to tell them *everything* I knew. In one breath! At the end of a one-to-one training session, I'd send the owner reams of follow-up notes. *You can do this . . . and then you can do that . . . once you've done that, then move on to the other . . . and pleeease like me!* The information was correct, but there was far, far too much of it. I knew what I was talking about, but it was overwhelming for the clients. So overwhelming, in fact, that I doubt it was ever put into practice.

I think dogs are like humans in this respect. When owners rabbit on at their dogs, the dog has two choices: respond to everything or respond to nothing. In dog training, owners who use their words wisely and economically are more successful. They end up with a dog that listens out for and hears every verbal cue as something precious to convert. The owner who drones on and on unfortunately loses the potentially precious cues amongst all of the jumbled, less valuable words. The lid that fits gets lost amongst all of the other Tupperware lids.

If you give an owner one or, at a push, two things to put into practice after a dog training session, they'll do it. They'll receive their own reinforcement for a job well done and they'll come back for more. If you give an owner ten things to do, there will be a log jam and they'll do nothing. They'll get no reinforcement and the practice sessions will become extinct. Everyone's a loser. The right advice and the right *amount* of advice are two different things.

After about ten years of me throwing the entire contents of my brain at any poor dog owner within range, I had earned enough money to upgrade my rubbish dog van to a slightly less rubbish dog van. As I cleared out my old van before the part exchange, I must have emptied out a hundred tennis balls, fifteen dog bowls, thirty leads, twenty collars, a thousand dog-poop bags (some still unused), and dozens of blankets, coats and hats. You name it, it came out of that van. Most of it had remained unused for so long, it was now useless: damp, mouldy, rotten. I had a favourite lead, one water bowl and a couple of dog toys that I always used. The rest was redundant, ballast at best.

When I got my new van, I swore only to have on board those items I actually used: one lead, one long line, one bowl, my favourite two toys, and so on. I had everything I ever needed to hand, which meant I never again had to sort through tons of junk to get to what I was looking for. I never

AMBER

again had to abandon a search for the relevant kit because there were messy piles of junk that needed negotiating.

I realised that what was true in my van was true in other parts of my life. In future, the follow-up reports and training plans that I sent to owners would be ready not when there was nothing left to add, but when there was nothing left to remove. I became Mister Succinct.

Mr S.

I had spent twenty years adding more and more to my dog trainer's toolbox. Conversely, the rest of my life (to date, I'm not dead yet!) has been spent jettisoning the redundant in order to become more streamlined, efficient and effective.

Ask any builder to show you his toolbox (oh, grow up) and I reckon he'll confirm that he only really uses 20 per cent of what he lugs around on a daily basis. The rest goes rusty. I guess it's important that we kiss a few frogs before we each find our prince. We might lug around a few hundred dog leads or spanners or techniques before we realise what works best for us, but the valuable and often brave thing to do is that once we realise what is most effective, we free ourselves of the unimportant baggage. And if you're currently thinking, *Wow, is this a brilliant metaphor for *insert chaotic part of my life** then I'm here to agree: it *is* a brilliant metaphor! If we're going to be effective, we need also to be efficient.

ANOTHER DAY, ANOTHER COLLAR

So what about the Tupperware? Well, we had so much of it that we were unable to use any of it. So I threw it all out, bought just two containers with matching lids and we now use both every day.

🐾

Sometimes in my own career, I'd get a little like Sally. I'd arrive at a crossroads with so many questions that I'd feel hamstrung into not knowing what to do. Perhaps it was a job offer I was unsure of, or I was struggling to gather the confidence to go after a particular role, or I was not sure how to deal with a particularly awkward customer.

Originally, I thought the role of being a dog trainer was just teaching dogs and their owners, but no, that's not the half of it. I discovered that if I wanted to survive as a professional trainer, I also had to be a secretary, a marketeer, a social worker, a shoulder to cry on, an accountant, a hustler, a motivator, an entertainer, a poo picker, a dog walker, a tea maker, a tidy-upper and an optimist. And only then did I need to be good with dogs.

With so many hats to wear but access to so few others who had done what I set out to do and become a dog trainer, my biggest problem was that I had no one to turn to if I wanted to ask for advice.

Or did I?

With an often-times disconcertingly childish imagination, I figured out that, amazingly, I could have immediate

AMBER

access to any mentor in the world I wanted. Even now, those lines of communication are permanently open.

You can do it too if you want.

Here's the plan. Take a piece of paper and a pen, and write down the issue you'd like to address. Describe the problem in five bullet points. Use no more than half the page.

Once you've written down the five bullet points of your predicament, you're going to read them out aloud.

Now, you'll need to be honest. You'll realise that whereas the first three points may be valid conundrums, numbers four and five are likely to be a thin soup. You can discount those bad boys straight away. Put a line through them.

So now you have three bullet points holding you back from committing to a decision.

Cool. Ask your mentor. It's as simple as that.

What?

You don't have a mentor?

But you *do* have a mentor.

You have eight billion mentors. If you feel that you don't have access to one right now, I'll happily share some of mine with you. Here are five of my mentors, who I've always been happy to run my problems past:

Paul McCartney

Pablo my Staffie

Scrappy Doo

Cool Hand Luke

Me in thirty years' time

ANOTHER DAY, ANOTHER COLLAR

If I'm stuck at a crossroads, I'll jot down my five points, dismiss two, then ask advice of one of my mentors. Stuck on a decision between heart and head? Paul McCartney will make sure I go with my heart and he'll want me to take the path that shares as many benefits as possible with others. He'll make sure I'm of service to others, and he'll make sure I'm kind. Two offers of work? Pablo my Staffie will want me to do whichever is the most fun. Life is for the living! Worried about what others will think of me or my choices? Scrappy Doo will straighten that one out quick smart. Let me at 'em! Need to check my moral compass? Cool Hand Luke will have the solution. 'Calling it your job don't make it right, Boss.'

By far your most important mentor, though, is you in thirty years' time. Do you have a relationship, career or any other decision to make right now? Jot it down, imagine you're speaking to yourself in thirty years' time and run it past that person. They'll know exactly how important it is or, more often, isn't. They'll let you know what to do. Me in thirty years' time is fairly consistent with his advice. Get on with it, mate. Have a go. Life's too short and the world's not waiting for you. We're diddy little specks of dust on another speck of dust zooming around the universe with loads of other little specks of dust.

So ask your mentor, then get on with it.

Chump

In my mission to accept all work offers that involved dogs, as a tactic to avoid signing up for what my mum *still* calls a 'real job', in 2001, I returned a call from a TV researcher on the show *Big Brother's Little Brother*.

This was the companion show to its older, better-known sibling *Big Brother*, which was a huge hit at the time and the daddy of reality TV. They wanted a trained dog who would somehow predict that week's eviction victim. The idea was that the dog, stage name Mr Chips, would head over to a big wicker basket, pull out one of the many scrolls of paper that held the names of the individual *Big Brother* housemates and deliver the randomly selected scroll to the show's presenter Dermot O'Leary, who would be sat waiting on the settee. Dermot would take the scroll from the dog's mouth and announce – drumroll please – the Eviction Prediction.

On paper, and in the eyes of the scriptwriters at least, this was a fairly simple activity for the dog to perform. In reality, it would require a hell of a lot of training. I would need to teach the dog to be comfortable and happy in the TV studio, with lots of people shuffling around in the dark, an unusually shiny floor, the lights, the cameras, the action. I would need to teach the dog to be comfortable with Dermot. I would need to teach the dog to be stationary in one position on the studio floor, away from me, as they waited for their cue. This might be quite some period of time as we waited for everything to be in place, the Channel 4 ads to finish and the section to start. When cued by Dermot with an 'Away you go, Mr Chips!' (what's called a 'sendaway') the dog would need to head towards the basket, pick up a scroll in their mouth, return to Dermot, jump up onto the settee, release the scroll into Dermot's hands and wait on the settee next to him while he read out the prediction to the studio audience. And finally, when Dermot said, 'Off you go, Mr Chips,' the dog would have to hop from the couch and head towards me, off camera.

So: simple on paper. In reality, there were over ten behaviours to teach in one long behaviour chain, all to be delivered in one go, and – oh yeah – all on live TV! They clearly needed a great dog trainer to deliver such a feat. And they'd clearly spent the previous three weeks calling all the great dog trainers on their list, with no joy.

So the poor sods were left with nothing but my number and forty-eight hours' notice.

True to my oath to accept all jobs that included dogs, I grabbed the opportunity.

The beauty of this gig was that the show was filmed at Elstree Studios, Hertfordshire. The George Lucas studio, to be exact. It just so happened that these studios were only twenty minutes' drive from my home at the time. So, with the show being filmed live, and the Eviction Prediction piece being done at the beginning of the hour-long show, even if it all went terribly wrong, I could gather up the dog, drive home, change my name, destroy my phone, have plastic surgery and bury myself in my back garden before the broadcast was even over.

The dog I trained for the show was an amazing little character called Teddy, a robust Cairn terrier I borrowed from my good friends Helen and James. Thankfully, Teddy was a star. We practised like billy-o for the forty-eight hours we had before showtime and I called the producer to request – nay, insist – that we could go into the studio as much as possible in advance of filming, so I could train, cue and reinforce the desired behaviours from Teddy in the actual location where we were going to need them.

Dermot O'Leary, also a young buck at the time, was blinding. A really nice fella, exactly the same off camera as he was on camera. He was super friendly, loved Teddy and, like me, had a long family heritage back in Ireland. What's not to love? Thankfully, the piece with Mr Chips was successful and went on to become a regular section for every *Big Brother's Little Brother* Friday episode.

I began to get more and more comfortable in TV land. I loved being on set to see the furious swan legs that erratically kick under the surface to generate the elegance we punters see at home on the box. The catering is normally pretty good as well, and it's free! That's not to say I didn't have more misses than hits when it came to converting telly opportunities. I remember once doing a screen test for a dog TV show. Word came back that the decision-makers weren't too sure about me. They thought I was a little too laid back, insufficiently 'up for it'. They wanted me back a week later to do another screen test, but this time they wanted me *pumped*.

No problem. I understood conditioning, pairing emotions to certain triggers. I do this for a living, mate!

What I did was simple: I got right into the movie *Rocky*. I watched the training montages time and time again. I downloaded the soundtrack onto my iPod and listened to it day and night. I could feel my testosterone rise as I slept. I *was* the Eye of the Tiger! On the tube journey into town for my second screen test, I listened to the soundtrack yet again, a little too loud perhaps. I was *so* pumped by the time the show's runner politely invited me into the room, I was ready to rip someone's head off!

'A little too aggressive for us,' came the rejection note from the broadcaster.

Fair comment. Perhaps I'd over-clubbed the conditioning this time around. In my defence, this is a good tool to have in your back pocket if you want to be able to draw upon an emotion on tap. I know it works because hundreds of dogs have shown me that it does. Of course, what goes on around us will influence how we feel, but how we feel will also influence what goes on around us. I had a period when if I was feeling optimistic, happy or excited, I'd deliberately listen to 'New York City' by John Lennon. I've paired the tune to the happy and optimistic feelings enough times that if I'm about to do an interview or a presentation, a quick listen to that song means I'm all set to go, smiling and feeling positive about my next step.

You'll already have a tune that you can call upon. Think of the music you used to listen to as a teenager in your bedroom on a Friday night as you were getting ready to go out with your mates. That's your very own 'New York City' right there. Don't waste the positive associations that you've cultivated for yourself in the past. Be like a dog and use them to activate joy for yourself and others around you. It's what Lennon would've wanted. I Imagine.

In late 2006, I was given the heads-up that the BBC had a new dog training show in the pipeline and to expect a call for an audition. *The Underdog Show* was to be a live competition in front of a studio audience where ten celebrities were to be paired up with ten professional dog trainers, who would each choose a rescue dog from a Dogs Trust rescue centre. The teams would then compete weekly around a dog obstacle course to show off their previous week's worth of training. The combined scores of three panel judges plus the voting public at home were added up, and the lowest scoring team each week was eliminated from the competition. Brutal.

The production was auditioning for trainers to join the show and asked if I'd be happy to send them a video of one of my classes. Was this what I wanted to do? I consulted my mentors. Paul McCartney, Pablo the Staffie, Scrappy Doo, Cool Hand Luke and me in thirty years' time were unanimous: go for it!

ANOTHER DAY, ANOTHER COLLAR

The production team told me not to set up anything special, just to film one of my *usual* classes.

Sod that!

I gathered the very best dogs and owners from all of my classes and put together a ten-minute demo class that would have had Doctor Doolittle taking notes.

Video submitted and tension loaded, I waited two nervous weeks before getting the call from the casting director offering me the job. 'You'll be working with Selina,' they said.

'Ah, fab!' I replied, 'fab' being TV talk for 'good'. I proceeded to rack my brains trying to work out who 'Selina' was. The only Selina I was aware of at the time was a character in *Home and Away* (what can I tell you, professional dog trainers keep irregular working hours), but surely she wouldn't be coming all the way from Oz for the show. And also, Selina was the character's name, not the actress's. It turns out that I wasn't to be paired with the antipodean actress, but with the English national treasure Selina Scott.

A quick history lesson for the teenagers: Selina was first a household name in the 1980s. In addition to presenting such staples as *Breakfast Time* in 1983 (little Steve: 'Damn, I've got to go to school in five minutes . . .') and Sunday evening's *The Clothes Show* in 1986 (slightly bigger but still not happy Steve: 'Damn, I've got to go to school tomorrow . . .'), Selina Scott had interviewed everyone who was anyone: all the royals, Bono, Donald

Trump. But with me being a Beatles nut, I asked her about the time she met George Harrison every single day we worked together.

I thought the TV show was a great idea. Not only would it beam dog training fun and entertainment into British living rooms, it also massively promoted the joy to be had from taking on a rescue dog, as well as putting ten lucky dogs into the spotlight, all of whom would be snapped up by loving homes before the series had even ended. Result!

For the first day's filming I was to meet my designated celebrity and we were to walk the line of kennels at the Dogs Trust rescue centre in Harefield, west London to choose the dog we'd like to work with for the duration of the series. I felt like I was meeting the Queen when first introduced to Selina in front of the cameras. She was super friendly, but so posh that I didn't know whether to bow, curtsey or throw my fleece across a puddle for her to walk over. I suffer from a terrible working-class affectation whereby the posher the person I meet, the more I weirdly counter their polished pronunciations by becoming increasingly cockney. It's not deliberate – I guess I'm trying to pull the graphic equaliser down to an average reading I'm more comfortable with – but if one day I could muster the confidence to speak to the landed gentry without doing a poor impression of Danny Dyer in the Queen Vic on Jubilee Day, strike a light, that'd be 'andsome.

Followed by lights and cameramen, Selina and I entered the stark, sterilised tiled environs of the kennel block – not unpleasant, but certainly more hygiene than hygge – to walk the line of ten kennels and choose our dog for the competition. 'How about this chap?' Selina said as we stopped outside the first kennel. It housed a Jack Russell who I can only describe as having a thousand-yard stare. Now, being a dog training pro, I like to be able to support my opinions with science, fact and all of that good, robust, nailed-on supportive evidence. But this guy? He had demons. I could feel it in my gut. This was Casper, who was chosen to team up with Huey Morgan, of Fun Lovin' Criminals fame. Casper was a great choice for Huey. I could imagine the pair of them under a bridge at night in 1980s New York, huddled around a flaming brazier, singing a cappella while Huey bounced a baseball in leather fingerless gloves and steam rose from the drain covers. A lovely little match-up, but I knew that this particular little Jack Russell wasn't winning any competitions.

The second kennel was more promising. A huge doofus of a dog came straight up to his kennel door and rubbed against it for cuddles. Dear reader, meet Chump. I've met many dogs in my life who have served as lighthouses for me as I've negotiated choppy waters. Believe me, Chump proved to be one of the biggest and brightest. A cross between a German shepherd and an Irish wolfhound? Yes, please! 'This is the dog for us,' I said to Selina

'You've another eight kennels to check first, Steve,' said the director.

'No, thank you,' I replied. 'We're good.'

CHUMP

'Are you sure?' Selina asked. I promised her that Chump was the one for us. In just a few seconds, I had seen that he was optimistic and happy to be with people.

'What about the earlier chap?' said Selina, walking back towards kennel one and Casper. I swiftly opened Chump's kennel, popped a lead on him and walked with him into the next, so much brighter, chapter of his life.

'Come on, Selina,' I said. 'We've work to do!'

Once outside, Selina and I took Chump into an enclosed paddock to let him off lead for a run and for the three of us to get to know each other. As Chump romped around the paddock like a horse that had thrown his jockey just for kicks, Selina completely stumped me: 'What do we do if he eliminates?'

Eliminates? 'Don't worry,' I said, 'the paddock's fully enclosed, he won't get out.'

'No,' said Selina. 'What if he . . . *eliminates*?'

Then it hit me. 'If he craps, you mean? Well, we pick it up.' I handed her a fistful of poo bags and subtly stepped back, leaving her closest to the potential crime.

Niceties exchanged and ice broken, I left Chump and Selina in the paddock as I was dragged away to do my first pre-competition interview on camera. 'So, Steve, what do you think your chances are with Selina and Chump?'

'Honestly? It's in the bag,' I said, remembering what my dad had said to me when I was a kid about why he loved greyhounds: because they always try their best. 'Try your best,' Dad would say, 'or not at all.'

ANOTHER DAY, ANOTHER COLLAR

I've heard other parents say similar to their kids, but the intention behind it is the polar opposite. '*Just* try your best,' they say. That 'just' is there to reduce personal responsibility. It's like when Elvis Presley and Frank Sinatra each covered Paul McCartney's 'Yesterday'. The original lyric takes responsibility and admits 'I said something wrong, now I long for yesterday', but when macho Elvis and Sinatra had a go, they changed it to 'I *must have* said something wrong' to pass the buck! '*Just* try your best' is a mealy mouthed, get-out-of-jail caveat for *not* trying your best. It's there as a bouncy castle to soften the blow of the expected loss. I didn't want a *just* to fall back on. Losing bloody hurts me, but not as much as knowing that I'm not genuinely trying my best. I wish I could say I'm fuelled by the joy of winning but, honestly, I'm not. It's the opportunity of trying my best multiplied by the pain of losing that gets me out of bed an hour earlier than my competitors if I decide to be in it to win it.

The show was broadcast live at 8pm each week in front of a studio audience and was presented by Julian Clary. I know, right? The three esteemed judges were Kay Lawrence, Peter Purves (formerly of *Blue Peter*, who I always confused with the Green Cross Code man) and Annie Clayton. Other celebrities on the show, in addition to Huey Morgan, included *Strictly*'s Anton Du Beke and Clive Anderson, plus Theo Paphitis of *Dragon's Den* and TV presenter Kirsty Gallagher.

CHUMP

One of the other trainers – let's call him Danny the Dog to save his blushes – had absolutely zero time for me. Good ol' DTD was, as we used to say back in my Walthamstow days, a little too chippy to liaise with the likes of me. When the VT of me saying 'It's in the bag' was used in the first show, the only thing Danny the friggin' Dog ever said to me after that was a sneering, 'It's in the bag, is it?' each time I entered the green room or he walked past with any of the crew. Plum.

Five days before each show, we were given the plan for the competition course that the teams were expected to complete. Most of the other teams met up to train two or three times a week. Selina, Chump and I would train at least twice a day. I figured that when Chump wasn't with us, he was back in his kennels. That in itself was reason enough to have him out so we could spend more time together. There was another reason, though: I wanted to try my best to win, and Selina, thank the stars, was just as competitive as me.

Whereas the others started their training by immediately trying to get their dogs over jumps, around poles and through tunnels, my tactic was simpler: to teach Chump that it was in his interest to follow Selina. That's the foundation of all my training, whether it's a pet dog, a detection dog or a security dog. If your dog doesn't want to hang out with you, good luck with anything else. I taught Selina simply to say 'Good' and pop a treat into Chump's mouth each time he glanced at her. Guess what? He soon learned to love looking at her! Once he was checking in with Selina when they were stationary, I'd ask her to start walking slowly and if Chump, through his own agency, chose to follow and glance at her, she'd return the compliment with a 'Good' and then give him the treat. Now, as they walked towards an agility jump, Chump would pop over it alongside Selina in order to follow the path of least resistance to his next treat, which was never too many strides away.

I wanted to do what the other teams weren't prepping for: to perform the tricks in front of a live studio audience. To that end, we maintained the reinforcement for checking in on the move, but we very quickly transferred it from the training room to the busy Dogs Trust reception, the car park and even to the high street. Then we brought it back to the training room, but at night with the lights off, as I played crowd noises on a stereo and flashed a torch around the room, to simulate the studio atmosphere. Chump didn't have to practise making changes to the behaviour he'd learned. He just had to remain consistent while we played around making changes to the environment during training.

So many people think they've taught their dog a behaviour by practising it a hundred times in the kitchen and are surprised when it all goes out the window down at the park. My tip is to teach fewer behaviours but in more environments. It's called 'proofing' the behaviour and it's not sufficiently considered in many walks of life. It's why the school play read-through goes well but then feels a bit funky at the dress rehearsal.

CHUMP

The day of the first show arrived and many of the other trainers and celebrities suddenly seemed a little less friendly. Cool. Game on! In the afternoon, each team had fifteen minutes on the studio floor to run through the course of jumps and hoops and God knows what else we were to be challenged with. I watched each team. As soon as the judges shouted 'Go!', invariably the handler went one way and the dog went the other. And why wouldn't they? I always try to figure out why a dog will or won't exhibit a particular behaviour by considering what *I* would do if placed in a similar situation. The other teams were expecting their dogs to walk from outside daylight straight into a dark, oddly lit, intriguingly smelling studio, and perform a specific and, let's be honest, unnatural series of behaviours, without first allowing them to do a few safety checks, bed in and feel comfortable with the environment and equipment. I'm the kind of guy who, when visiting a nightclub, would need to do a walk of the perimeter first and become relaxed and feel safe before the dance moves are released. Even today, I have to sit with my back to the wall in a restaurant (my early career in security dog handling planted that particular paranoid seed, making me hyper-vigilant, always looking for the bad guy before looking for the good guy). Remember, survival is so much more important than obedience, for all of us.

When Selina, Chump and I entered the arena for our pre-show rehearsal, I simply asked Selina to unclip Chump from his lead and let him mooch around the stage.

ANOTHER DAY, ANOTHER COLLAR

Of course, Chump flew around the course looking and sniffing at all the freshly painted props and obstacles. Everything was so new to him; it was like stepping from a spaceship onto Mars for the first time. Expecting specific behaviours straightaway would be like asking a kid to do their eight times tables as soon as they set off on their first rollercoaster ride. Just not gonna happen.

Once Chump had bedded in and checked under all of the equipment for cats, food or villains, he started to check in with Selina – and when he did: 'Good' and treat, 'Good' and treat . . . His curiosity for the environment soon diminished, but his appetite for Selina's goodies remained strong. And when showtime arrived, Chump aced it.

As the weeks went by and a team was eliminated each episode, the true value of the show became apparent. The viewing public became aware of rescue dogs and the amazing centres that support them, and were turned on to the prospect of rehoming a rescue dog, rather than buying from a conveyor belt of breeders. All of the dogs participating in the show went on to be rehomed by loving families before the series run was complete. And I've no doubt that thousands more dogs from rescue centres went on to find their forever homes partly because their new owners had seen the show.

After several shows, we arrived at the final episode. The runners and riders were Selina with Chump, Huey Morgan with Casper and actor Julia Sawalha with Cookie, a cute little Staffie. For the final freestyle round, we asked wardrobe to make Chump a Superman cape which we attached to a collar. As part of their obstacle course, Chump entered an agility tunnel and as he exited, his head went through the collar and he emerged wearing his Superman cape. The amazing Chump and the equally amazing Selina were the winners. From Chump to Champ. Get in!

When Julian Clary awarded the huge trophy to Selina, I was brought on to the stage for our victory lap. My mates still take the rise out of me now for embracing and kissing Chump to celebrate, while completely ignoring the radiant Selina Scott.

Chump went on to live a long and loving life with a beautiful couple in Cornwall, who kindly kept me up to date with constant photos of his happily ever after. I learned so much from him. He was full of optimism and when he had his opportunity, he grabbed it with both paws. He was always up for a laugh and he was always affectionate. He was everything I wanted to be.

I was buzzing when, at the end of the show's after party with all of the cast and crew, Selina graciously gave me the trophy to take home. As I loaded the trophy into the back of my van, who should I see on the other side of the car park but our dear old friend Danny the Dog.

'Hey, Danny,' I shouted.

He looked around in the dark and his eyes finally landed on me. 'What?'

'It's in the bag, baby!'

Alfa Animal Crew

After hanging on to Chumps coattails for series one of *The Underdog Show*, I was asked to be one of the esteemed judges on the panel for series two. This was to be the first, and admittedly the last, time I got to wear a suit for work. Among the competitors of series two were Brian Blessed and the rescue dog Dougal, a pointer crossed with a bearded collie. Of course he was crossed with a bearded collie if he was going to partner up with Brian Blessed!

Brian and I struck up quite the friendship. I adored the way he lived life to the full. He was a kindred spirit who also subscribed to a philosophy of committing all-in or all-out. He demonstrated that commitment to me one lunchtime on set. As the first course arrived, he was telling me with pure delight how he conquered Everest and how he would go out jogging with the soldiers from the military base opposite his home on a regular basis, despite him being well into his seventies. Mid-course, as I was telling a story of my own, I looked up from buttering my bread and my words faded to silence as I saw that Brian was sound asleep. Snoring.

None taken, mate. None taken.

Another TV gig I've done a good few times is *BBC Breakfast*. On one particular occasion, I was invited onto

ANOTHER DAY, ANOTHER COLLAR

the red couch to discuss the prospect of a new American company that had set up a 'dogs for hire' scheme, where people who didn't want to commit full-time to a dog would rent one for perhaps a weekend or a trip away. I always try to be on the bright, cheery, cheeky chappie, positive side of things. But to be honest, my position was a big fat resounding: 'You're kidding, right?' I didn't like the idea of dogs being seen as disposable commodities for short weekends, then dumped back when the consumer was done with them. Believe it or not, though, that wasn't the main thing that got my back up that morning.

In all of these daytime TV pieces, the producers try to pitch a 'for' guest opposite an 'against' guest, then sit back to watch conflict ensue. The researchers were well aware that I was firmly ensconced in the 'against' corner, so they needed to find me a worthy nemesis. For some reason, unknown to me to this day, my opponent in the opposite corner was high-kicking and even higher-falutin' star of *Strictly Come Dancing* Anton Du Beke. I can only think Anton was placed on the couch opposite me because of his previous experience on series one of *The Underdog Show*.

I'm always up for a friendly chat about dogs, but what raised my hackles that morning (in addition to the alarm clock going off at 4am) was that Anton constantly referred to Ginger, the dog he had worked with on *The Underdog Show*, as 'it'. He also said that people may own a dog but then say, 'Oh, I've got to go back to work now, what am

I going to do with this?' *This*? A dog is not a 'this', mate! He said, 'The trouble is, you can get attached to the things.' The *things*?

I'm being horribly harsh on Anton here to illustrate a point. He's a nice guy. He wasn't a 'dog person' at the time, but I'm happy to say that he really is now. But when it comes to how we refer to dogs, words really matter. To label a dog as an 'it', 'thing' or 'this' is a real bugbear of mine. I know these are not uncommon terms used for dogs, but they bloody well should be. Dogs are amazing, sentient, generous living beings. If you ever hear a dog trainer in real life or on social media referring to a dog as an 'it' or a 'this', then they just don't get it. Walk away, delete and seek compassion elsewhere.

A few years later, I was invited to be involved with a new TV show for Sky called *Pet Nation*, which was to be filmed at the BBC's Shepherd's Bush Studios. Initially, a pilot was filmed, and I think the bigwigs weren't particularly impressed as following the pilot a meeting was called, which everyone involved in the pilot was summoned to attend. We all sat around a large oval boardroom table and were introduced to the new producer, who was clearly determined to be a new brush, sweeping clean. I was told that, in addition to presenting some onscreen pieces and generating VTs about dogs and training, I was also to be the show's 'animal consultant'. It was explained to me that the role of the animal consultant was to be on set for all rehearsals and recordings, with the responsibility of ensuring that all health and safety and welfare concerns were avoided or addressed for all the animals passing through the wide studio doors, not just the dogs. That meant cats, rabbits, snakes, horses, cows, goats, guinea pigs, gerbils . . . you name it, they were going to have it, and ol' Muggins here was the man they wanted to ensure that all went smoothly or to take full responsibility and accept all liability when the horse swallowed the dog that swallowed the cat that swallowed the parrot that swallowed the gerbil, I don't know why . . .

I was way out of my comfort zone. So of course, I said yes.

'In addition . . .' the producer said.

'What, in addition to doing the risk assessment for Noah's Ark?'

She ignored the joke.

'In addition, your role as animal consultant will include booking *all* of the animals needed for the show.'

Bloody hell, I thought. *That's going to be a problem.*

'Great,' I said. 'No problem at all!'

'On Mondays,' she said, 'we'll email you the list of all the animals required, and you'll have forty-eight hours to book them from your animal supply agencies in order for them to be on set for rehearsals and filming.'

My 'animal supply agencies'? Either she had the wrong guy or she thought I had a lot more contacts than I did. On the drive home, I was in a right old state, my mind racing as I worried that I was going to lose the job. They'd be

ALFA ANIMAL CREW

wanting five to ten animals per show, and I only had access to my own dogs. I mean, it was awesome that they had a budget for each animal, but what the hell is an animal supply agency?

With necessity being the mother of invention, and this at least being an opportunity to try my best, by the time I had completed my forty-five-minute drive home from Shepherd's Bush studios, I had decided that if all of these funds were going to be heading to a third-party agency, then yours truly would be the third party agency! I had come up with a name – Alfa Animal Crew (sounded legit to me) – called my mate to set up a website for it, and called my other mate who still worked in the same Barclays Bank branch that I had started at to set up a bank account. I called the show's production manager, who wanted to agree a set fee for any animal, regardless of species, so they could bake the costs into their budget. I laid it on thick that the costs involved in getting a horse or cow safely to the studio would be huge. With a bit of back and forth, they agreed to average out the set fee to £500 per animal. Great, I told them, brimming with temporary chutzpah. I was confident that I could negotiate and get the agency *winks to camera* to agree to such demands.

Fast forward a couple of weeks and the show goes into production. I'm good with most animals but like any sane person, I'm afraid of snakes. No reasonable person *isn't* afraid of snakes. So you can guess the first animal they wanted me to source from the 'animal supply agency'. For episode one they wanted a snake so the show could demonstrate safe snake-handling techniques. They also wanted six gerbils to demonstrate a racing-car-shaped exercise ball. They wanted to build a track in the studio, so the six gerbils could bomb around it with commentary provided by sports commentator Mark 'Chappers' Chapman – he's on *Match of the Day* now, but this was back when we were both clearly scraping a living . . .

As I was a part-time lecturer of an animal care college at the time, I popped into their reptile section and, if I'm ever challenged in court, I *asked* if I could borrow the college corn snake, Your Honour. Of course, with me being a scaredy cat, I got one of the college students to place the snake in the carrier. When I got to the studio, I lucked out: one of the show's runners was right into snakes, so he asked if he could do all of the snake handling backstage. Being the big-hearted and generous old softy that I am, I gave that runner his first leg-up in TV, allowing him to take my role and do all the snake handling on screen as well. I know, right?

For the gerbils, I popped in to see my mate who ran a pet shop. They cost £8 each. So I gave him his money on the Tuesday, did the filming on the Wednesday and the gerbils were back in store by Thursday night. Even I had to squint when Alfa Animal Crew Ltd made out its first invoice for 7 x £500. Three and a half grand on top of my

ALFA ANIMAL CREW

normal fee for a borrowed snake and forty-eight quid's worth of gerbils! *I'll never have to get a real job at this rate*, I thought, and I was right.

Each week the orders came in from the production office for me to pass on to the agency (tee hee). And each week the orders were satisfied by hook or by crook. Each week the Alfa Animal Crew Ltd invoices were paid upon receipt. What a time to be alive!

The presenters of the show were Liza Tarbuck – a very funny lady – and my old friend from series one of *The Underdog Show*, Mr Huey Morgan. It was great to hook up with him again. Similar to my wolf-from-the-door angle with the Alfa Animal Crew agency, Huey's rider for each show was a super-expensive bottle of Japanese whiskey. A bottle a show! He wouldn't touch the whisky in the room, but each night he would pop it into his holdall before bowling into his Addison Lee and making out like a bandit. He must have had a cellar like Oliver Reed's by the end of the run. As we sat in his dressing room each night pre-show, Huey would tell me about his old pit bull Sugar, who he lived with when he was younger, back home in New York. He even wrote something of a love song to her, titled 'Sugar', which you can hear on the Fun Lovin' Criminals second album, *100% Columbian*.

In addition to the larger shows, I've also had the pleasure of being on *Loose Women* (grow up!) and have appeared as a guest on Gabby Logan's chat show along with Irish comedian Sean Hughes and glamorous Italian lawyer and socialite Nancy Dell'Olio. Here's a little competition for you. Have a look at the picture below.

Now guess which of the three guests spent two hours in makeup and which two didn't bother. Good luck!

I've also been a guest a few times on ITV's *Lorraine* show, hosted by the lovely Lorraine Kelly, who was nothing but supportive and really helped with the promotion of my first book *Easy Peasy Puppy Squeezy*. One of my favourite people to work with was Ashleigh Butler, who won *Britain's Got Talent* with her special dog Pudsey. Ashleigh and I presented a show for CBBC called *Who Let The Dogs Out?*, a dog training show to encourage kids to do more with their dogs. It was such a lovely programme to work on, and all filmed from the manor house at Arley Gardens in Cheshire – the same swanky house that was used later by *Peaky Blinders* as the home of the Shelby family. Iconic, sure, but Ashleigh and I got there first.

Once I started to move within the la-di-dah circles of TV, I was often asked by some big names to help them with the training of their own dogs. One such celebrity was Graham Norton. I would meet up with him in Hyde Park to train him and his beautiful rescue labradoodle Bailey. I did several sessions with Graham and Bailey and we got on really well. And let's just say that, after a few sessions, Bailey smashed through fewer picnics in Hyde Park than he did before we first met.

Around the period I was seeing Graham and his dog for training, I booked a weekend off – a rarity for me – as a gang of my mates were heading out for a stag weekend to celebrate my friend Jose's upcoming wedding. I lost the first bet, so I was the designated driver for day one. In high spirits, we headed down the M27 towards the coast for childish belly laughs and nonsense. As I was driving the car full of excited man-babies, an incoming text alert chimed on my phone. 'Get that for me, will you?' I said to my mate Ken who was in the front passenger seat.

He picked up my phone. 'It's from Graham Norton!'

'Wahay!' hollered the fully grown idiots from the back of the car.

'Shut up, everyone! What's it say?'

'Bloody hell!' exclaimed Ken. 'It says, "Do you have boy time for us this Friday?"'

More 'wahays' erupted from the back seat. As I tried

to grab the phone from Ken without crashing the car, the mobile was thrown to the back of the motor into the gaggle of – and I now use this term loosely – 'mates'. It was quite clear that predictive text had changed the innocent attempt to type 'any time' to a much more interesting 'boy time', leading to much hilarity. I tried to find somewhere to pull the car over. However, to my mortification, before I could park up, the hilarious chaps in the back had already rather unprofessionally replied to Graham on my behalf.

Thanks, chaps. Good job Graham's got a good sense of humour.

In 2010, I had a call from the BBC to go for an interview and audition for a show that was to be called *Over the Rainbow*. This was a live Saturday night primetime show, the format of which was a competition to discover a performer to appear as the star of the show, Dorothy, in Andrew 'The Lord' Lloyd Webber's *Wizard of Oz* production, set to be staged in London's glitzy West End. The show also ran a competition to find a dog to play the role of Toto alongside the newly cast Dorothy, and that's where I came in. I was asked to interview as one of the TV judges who would help discover Toto.

Following *The Underdog Show* and my other TV appearances, this gig was definitely one for me. I'm not normally confident when going for such interviews or auditions, but my past experience, paired with the fact that – and how's this for luck – the *Over the Rainbow* presenter was to be me old pal Graham Norton, the phrase 'a shoe in' came to mind.

I took the train into town to the offices of Talkback TV and was met by some of the glowing production crew at reception. As we rode the lift up to the meeting room, a member of the production team said to me, 'Graham's been telling us you train with him and his dog. That's awesome!'

'Yeah,' I said, already feeling part of the family. We exited the lift at the top floor and turned right to walk along the corridor, when who should be coming our way but my other old showbiz pal Dermot O'Leary.

'Steve!' he shouted from the far end of the corridor. 'How's it going, mate?' He came over to give me a big bear hug. 'How's Mr Chips?'

You beauty, I thought. With Graham Norton and Dermot O'Leary on my side, maybe they should just cut out the admin and show me where to sign. But no, we still had some hoops to jump through. 'We just need to do a little videotape of you,' said one of the production team, 'because although we think you're perfect for the role, Sir Andrew has to have the final sign-off.'

So with shoulders back and chest out, I did my piece to camera for the tape to be sent off to Balmoral, the Tower of London, or wherever it is that Andrew Lloyd Webber resides.

And within a week the results came back. Thanks, but no thanks.

Bloody hell, I thought that one was *definitely* in the bag. Lloyd Weber must have hated me!

What does he know about putting on a dog show anyway? He's clearly more of a *Cats* person.

In addition to TV, I really enjoy being on the radio, particularly when there's a chance to spend time digging into the topic of dogs, rather than concentrating on thirty-second soundbites. I've been a guest on BBC London a few times on a Sunday morning, when listeners would be invited to phone in to ask questions about their dogs. It was fun and hopefully good listening.

One particular Sunday morning, the show was to be hosted by Christopher Biggins. On the Saturday night, I made the mistake of mentioning it to my mates down the pub. Next morning, I leaned my head-phoned noggin in towards the mic as Christopher Biggins opened the phone-in. 'And we've got Andy here, who wants to talk to you about bringing his dog skiing.'

'Hi, Andy,' I said. 'You'll have to look into organising a pet passport for your dog to take them abroad, and make sure your dog is happy with the icy surface. Maybe consider boots for their feet in case the snow balls up between their toes—'

'No, no, sorry,' Andy interrupted. 'I want you to tell me

how to *teach* my dog to ski. I've bought the four little skis for each foot and I've had goggles made for him . . .'

The penny dropped. This wasn't some random Andy from the good old listening public. This was Andy, my mate from down the pub, gleefully roasting me live on air! And I kid you not, every bloody call that came into the show over that ninety-minute period was from someone who'd been down the pub with me the night before.

'Oh my goodness!' cried Biggins during the weather. 'The switchboard has lit up! We've never had so many calls.'

'Yeah,' I said. 'Terrific.' And I braced myself for the next caller, who sincerely wanted to know what he could do to change his dog's accent . . .

Nancy

As someone who works outside with dogs on a daily basis, covering many miles through parkland and woods, I'm constantly surprised and a little disappointed that I haven't yet discovered one of the dog walker's safari Big Five: a body, a briefcase full of cash, a kilo of coke, a gun or an injured fox to nurse back to health and become best friends with.

Sunday night BBC dramas have a lot to answer for.

I did, however, for one sweet moment believe that my dreams had come true the morning Gina returned to the bedroom at 6am, just as I was stirring from my golden slumbers, with a small animal gently wrapped in her arms. 'Look at what Mustafa has found for you,' she said.

Mustafa has been a dog training colleague of mine for several years. As he suffered both from living in south London *and* being extremely conscientious, he used to arrive to start work at my place – the training school where I was also living at the time – super early in order to avoid the traffic. I'd aim to start training dogs at ten each morning. Mustafa would arrive at six. Yay. Due to his frankly ridiculous habit of clocking in for work four hours early, Mustafa would pop into the nearby motorway service station for a coffee each morning on his way in. One day, as Mustafa was pulling into the service

ANOTHER DAY, ANOTHER COLLAR

station, he spotted a crazy little dog dodging in and out of the traffic. To save her life, he pulled over and scooped the little dog out of the road to safety. He then went into all the service station shops to ask if anyone had reported a missing dog, handed his mobile phone number to all the staff and reported the stray dog to the local dog warden in case they had received any distressed calls from a frantic owner. Then he headed to my place and passed the dog over for my attention.

As I blearily opened my eyes, sat up in bed and slowly drew focus, I would have bet a pound to a penny that this was it, the injured fox I'd been manifesting since I was a kid. Finally, albeit I was now in my forties, here was my chance to tick off one of the Big Five. As my vision cleared, however, I could see that this wasn't an injured fox at all but a diddly little teeny-weeny dog, maybe a chihuahua crossed with a terrier. She popped her head out from beneath the pink fleece blanket she'd been wrapped in, met my eyes and said, 'Wakey wakey, Sunshine, fancy a new adventure?'

We rang around all of the authorities, shops and offices at the service station and decided that the little dog would ride shotgun with me and my dog Carlos, a big Belgian shepherd, for the rest of the day until her family were tracked down, who must have been worried sick. Hopefully, they could be reunited with their pet and I'd be rewarded with a million pounds or a slap-up meal, just like in the *Beano*.

NANCY

Carlos and I went out for a walk together with the 'stray' that morning in the fields. I remember it well: dry summer, long grass swaying. As I walked behind the pair of them, I noticed that despite their maHOOOSive difference in size and stature, they somehow trotted together as a team, albeit at a different cadence. Sure, they were a piccolo and a big bass drum, but they were definitely from the same marching band. The little dog immediately fell into a comfy groove with me and Carlos. She naturally kept checking back to look to me while also sticking close to Carlos's side. Not only that, and I can't stress enough the importance of this, they were *exactly* the same colour. These things are important, you know, for the Instagram and such like.

I'd started the day falling in love with a fox that wasn't a fox, then calling anyone and everyone to get her off my hands. Now I was pondering, *Hmm . . . I wonder . . .*

I wanted her to be reunited with her original owners, didn't I? Of course I did. I'm not a monster! But, theoretically, it wouldn't be the end of the world, would it, if, you know . . . ('Theoretically' is how I always start to talk myself into taking on another rescue dog. As soon as I start using words like 'theoretically' or 'in principle', I know I'm done for.) As they marched to the sound of the same beat a couple of metres in front of me, this little dog looked like a spare jigsaw piece who had finally found her puzzle. Long lost twins. Schwarzenegger and DeVito.

After several more responsible calls that day, I eventually managed to track down her owners. It came to light that they had parked their caravan at the service station, were aware that their dog was loose and running around the traffic, and were aware that the dog had been picked up to prevent her from being run over or causing an accident. What they clearly weren't aware of, however, was that owning a dog is a real privilege. I decided to play hardball. Over the phone, I told them that they really should step up to look after her properly. I told them that I'd give them regular dog training lessons for free and that I'd also help them set up routines to keep her safe.

'Honestly,' I said, 'she's such a cracking little dog. Anyone would be lucky to have her.'

'No, they wouldn't,' came the reply.

'They would,' I said.

'Yeah? *You* have her then!' they said and hung up.

Oh. Looks like I'm gonna be a dad again.

First things first: a name for this new love of my life. Being a fan of the Beatles, I had a few female names to choose from. Lucy? Michelle? Penny? Even Rita was a possibility. In the end, though, I opted for a nod towards the Beatles song 'Bungalow Bill', so it wasn't long before 'everyone knew her as Nancy'. I also liked the *Oliver Twist*/Sex Pistols undertones. And that's how Nancy was born – or reborn, at least.

As with all of the dogs I've had the honour to share my life with, Nancy has taught me so much. I've trained thousands of dogs of all shapes and sizes, but up until this point I'd only ever lived with larger dogs. Living with a smaller dog, an itsy-bitsy teeny-weeny dog, is different. I don't mean they have specifically differing personality types compared to larger dogs, but the differences are apparent in normal day-to-day stuff, like their pace of movement. Small enthusiastic dogs move much faster than large enthusiastic dogs. It's simple mechanics. I'm well used to training dogs with a high drive, such as Belgian shepherds, but do the maths: a smaller dog is going to turn faster in a tighter circle than a bigger dog. Because of that awesome speed, your timing as a trainer needs to be on point or you'll have missed your opportunity to reinforce the desirable behaviours. Carlos was fast, but doing five minutes' training with Nancy and then going on to train Carlos was like water skiing behind a stolen speed boat, then hooking up behind a canal barge.

During those first few weeks living with Nancy, I found myself going into a blind panic at least three times a day as I thought I'd lost her during off-lead play because I struggled see her in the distance as easily as I would my larger dogs. You know that feeling when you call and chase, and you're trying to stay cool, but you notice that you start calling a little faster, your throat narrows and you can't help but morph into the kind of frantic character Dustin Hoffman becomes in the third act of every film he's ever been in. Chasing, looking, chasing, looking. Finally, I'd feel a little nudge on my ankle or foot, and look down to see Nancy looking back up as if to say, 'What? I've been here all the time, you muppet!'

ANOTHER DAY, ANOTHER COLLAR

After a couple of weeks, Nancy began to come out of her shell a little more – and let's just say she was not one for hiding her light under a bushel when it came to expressing herself. Little dog, big emotions. With the honeymoon period over, it was clear that Nancy struggled with unknown larger dogs coming up to her when she was on the lead. And when you're Nancy's size, all dogs are larger dogs. She would be desperate to put space between herself and the other dog. I'm guessing that in her previous life she was always on the lead (except when near motorways, clearly), as it seemed that she had learned that when under pressure from other dogs, as she couldn't run away to put distance between her and the perceived threat, the only way she could increase that distance was to tell the perceived threat, the other dog, to go away. How had she learned to 'tell' the other dog to go away, you ask? She went industrial: barking, spinning, lunging, jumping and snapping, all served on a generous bed of blood-curdling screams. She had a frantic pace of phrase that would have made a regimental sergeant major sound lethargic.

Nancy had been lucky enough to meet Carlos for the first time off lead. This had given her a sufficient window of opportunity to learn that he was a pretty cool older brother. It was the combination of being on the lead *and* approached by a strange dog that primed her to shoot first and ask questions later.

I call this behaviour rushing. On the face of it, rushing

NANCY

seems a counterproductive behaviour for a scared dog. It means going *towards* the scary thing, rather than *away* from it. In the natural world, we'd call this an extremely expensive or 'maladaptive' behaviour, as it comes with a high risk and a high energy expenditure. However, from Nancy's perspective, what else could she do when she felt unsupported and that this was her only option in a matter of life and death? And while it may seem odd to many, to me – someone who has learned to deal with the source of their discomfort by running towards it to slacken the tension – it makes perfect sense. The aggressive behaviour had worked for her in the past and had therefore become her default coping strategy when on the lead and faced with an unknown dog. Her barking and lunging would have resulted in the other dog wandering off murmuring, 'Okay, weirdo, I only wanted to sniff your butt,' or their owner walking away to reduce embarrassment. Failing that, the other dog may well have retaliated and attacked Nancy, only reinforcing to her that other dogs clearly *are* evil and that she'll need to get angrier sooner next time to get rid of the threat. The definitive vicious circle.

The contract I have with all of my dogs starts with my number one promise: 'I will keep you safe.' If my dogs feel safe, secure and optimistic, everything else is easier. If my dogs feel frightened or, worse still, that I'm not there for them, we're on very, very thin ice. With Nancy now firmly under my wing, my role was to teach her that she didn't have to face the world on her own anymore. That I had her back and if she ever felt it all getting a bit on top, I had her covered.

'Me & Nancy. Little dog, BIG emotions.'

My plan for Nancy was to set up a training programme of desensitisation and counter-conditioning. The desensitisation element involved me arranging set-ups with other dogs, in which Nancy and I were close enough to be aware of the other dog but not so close that Nancy would feel threatened in their presence.

We started the training by first employing the services of what we call a 'stooge' dog. A stooge dog is

NANCY

a nice passive, frankly boring dog that is calm in their movements and reliable in temperament. With the stooge dog first appearing to Nancy at a long distance away, and with him being stationary and standing sideways on, it was clear to Nancy that he posed no threat. I wanted Nancy initially to feel safe in the presence of a passive dog without her historic – and hysteric – Chicken Licken fear of the sky falling in on her. Over time, we decreased this distance, put a bit more movement into the stooge dog and changed his body position from sideways on to facing forwards, towards Nancy. Then we baked in some movement. Eventually, we transitioned on to other shapes, sizes, colours and sexes of stooge dogs, as well as gradually decreasing the distance between Nancy and the stooge, but always with an eye on Nancy's body language to ensure she continued to feel comfortable and secure.

I was trying to establish a foundation of safety and security for Nancy on which we could build. With this in place, we repeated similar set-ups in as many different environments as possible to generalise her sense of security. That was the desensitisation part. And to this, we introduced counter-conditioning. Nancy had previously learned that the presence of other dogs predicted potential bad news. You know as well as me that, when you're anticipating bad news, your breathing changes, your whole physiology goes a bit wonky and you get that horrible feeling in your gut. All of which contribute to shortening your fuse. It only takes the tiniest trigger to set you off.

ANOTHER DAY, ANOTHER COLLAR

The aim of Nancy's counter-conditioning programme was to turn that emotional response on its head. Rather than Nancy anticipating *bad* news in the presence of other dogs when she was on the lead, I wanted other dogs showing up to predict *good* news. That way, we could build Nancy's optimism and extend her tolerance. We could lengthen her fuse.

The counter-conditioning set-ups I did with Nancy in training started in a familiar location. With her on the lead, a stooge dog would appear as planned at a nice safe distance. I'd wait. Then, as soon as Nancy clocked her canine counterpart, phenomenal treats would rain from the sky for her. Once she had finished hoovering up the goodies, I waited until she looked at the dog and, as soon as she did, I'd say, 'Good,' and give her another treat. This would continue until the stooge dog walked away. And as soon as the other dog disappeared, so would the treats.

With enough repetition to engrain the favourable association, Nancy gained a positively conditioned emotional response to the presence of another dog because it predicted that dinner was to be served. Dog appears = food. Hurrah! Dog disappears = food stops. Boo! Bring back the stooge!

In addition, as a free bonus track, since the presence of another dog predicted food, not only did it help change the emotional response, it also presented us with a nice, cheap mutually exclusive behaviour, as Nancy learned to look up to me in anticipation of treats when she saw another

NANCY

dog (mutually exclusive because she couldn't look up at me and bark at the other dog at the same time). It was one of those special occasions where both Pavlov and Skinner can rest happy.

Forgive me for the following short intermission here, but I just want to say that I totally appreciate and empathise that all of this is so much easier, and certainly quicker, on paper than it is in the flesh. Working with dog-to-dog reactivity can be tough. It can feel like a long and bumpy road, but by letting your dog know that you have their back, and by following a route of sensible desensitisation and counter-conditioning, you'll get there. Measure your progress from where you were, not where you want to be. Have low targets, take the small wins and build from there. Remember, it's a process not an event. Training, like all new learning, takes time.

Nancy's training programme was designed to bring her from Tasmanian devil to at least being comfortable with other dogs. Of course, wedged between the initial wheel spinning and the gaining of traction, we lived in a period of damage limitation. A period where we were not yet where we wanted to be, but we didn't want to undo any work we had done to date or, worse still, take a massive backwards step due to a bad incident with another dog. In that interim period, I remained mindful of rule number one: keep Nancy feeling safe. We took all of our walks together in safe, secure locations at times of day when we were least likely to bump into other dogs. There's a clear distinction between controlled training set-ups and real life. I always want to teach my students a new language in a nice, clean, controlled classroom first. Only when I know they're fluent do I want them to show off their skills in a new landscape. If I parachute my student into a foreign land and put them under pressure to communicate before they can *parlez* the lingo, they'll panic and revert to their old familiar words when attempting to communicate. They won't improve, they'll just shout louder.

On top of walking in the least risky places, had we been ambushed by a dog heading towards us, I was categorically prepared to pick Nancy up to keep her safe and to get us out of Dodge with as little emotional damage as possible. A lot of owners (and dog trainers!) will jar at the thought of me telling people to pick up their dogs if they're uncomfortable around other dogs. There's a time-honoured but nonsensical theory that picking your dog up will 'make your dog worse' around other dogs.

I know. Bonkers, right?

Not keeping Nancy safe and teaching her that she had to keep monsters away on her own would have made her worse around other dogs. Don't forget: Nancy's tiny. She's living in the land of giants. Put yourself in her shoes. Her tiny, tiny little shoes. So if you're the owner of a small dog and they need you to pick them up for safety, bloody well pick them up! In fact, for the record, I don't care how big your dog is. I wouldn't be shy of slinging a Rottweiler over my shoulders to get out of trouble if

NANCY

they were struggling to cope with a perceived threat and needed my support.

Once we'd worked through Nancy's desensitisation and counter-conditioning, she became increasingly comfortable with other dogs, and with life in general. Remember when I told you that, since I'd mostly only ever been around larger dogs, I didn't have the habit of looking down to check in? Well, to remedy this, in addition to the eye contact, I taught Nancy that if ever she felt uncomfortable in the presence of other dogs and I didn't have my wits about me to spot this, she only had to put her two feet on my own foot. As soon as I felt her make contact, I'd lift her up, no questions asked. I'd love to explain how I did this, however, the master must teach the Jedi everything, except how to become the master.

I think dogs have been sent to me at my various life stages to teach me. I'm sure Pele the greyhound was sent to me in my twenties and thirties to teach me to chase and commit 100 per cent to reach my goals. You'll never see a greyhound chase anything half-heartedly, and you'll never see a greyhound sleep on a settee half-heartedly either! Pele taught me that I didn't need to live in fear of failure as I pursued my desire to work successfully with dogs. After I'd chased dog training job security like a loon for a decade or so, up popped Nancy to meet me in my forties to remind me that once we're safe and secure, we don't have to keep rushing, to keep chasing. Sometimes we need to pause to realise that what we need is standing right next to us.

Maggie

Imposter syndrome, anyone?

I'm sure it's not just me.

It used to be the first thud in my gut each morning before I even opened my eyes.

You're too young.

You're not qualified enough.

You don't have enough experience.

It's not a real job.

I'm sure many people in many walks of life have struggled with it. My argument is you'd be mad *not* to have it. Imposter syndrome is defined as *'a fear of criticism, doubting your abilities and feeling like a fraud. It disproportionally affects high-achieving people, who find it difficult to accept their accomplishments. Many question whether they're deserving of accolades.'*

To be fair, I think 'a fear of criticism, doubting your abilities and feeling like a fraud' is quite enough, but it tickles me that the rest of the definition turns into a kind of a humblebrag. 'Sure, I suffer from the old imp-syn. Why, it affects nearly all of us high achievers!' It's a bit like telling the job interviewer your greatest weakness is that, if anything, you work *too* hard.

Let's break imposter syndrome down and see what we can do with it. We'll start with 'fear of criticism'.

ANOTHER DAY, ANOTHER COLLAR

Is criticism something we need to fear? Here's a handy little exercise I've done in the past if I've ever caught myself feeling the effects of my efforts being criticised by *'cold and timid souls who neither know victory nor defeat'*, to quote Theodore Roosevelt. Choose a film, a book or an all-time great album that you adore, that you think is the best, that you think is awesome. Now go and search the internet to find some bad reviews. I promise you, they are out there. Just because these classics have their critics, does this mean they should never have been released or should now be ripped out of circulation in order to satisfy those critics? Of course not. And not least because critics will never be satisfied. They live to be unsatisfied. So let 'em.

Fear of criticism used to cripple me as a younger dog trainer but I've realised that it's impotent. In fact, to illustrate how impotent I believe it deserves to be, I'm more than happy to share some of the one-star reviews from Amazon for my first book *Easy Peasy Puppy Squeezy*.

> *I was expecting so much from this book given all the rave reviews, but 95% of what this (self-titled) expert recommends is contradictory or so badly delivered it's almost impossible to understand what he's advising the reader does. And don't get me started on the so-called humour.*

MAGGIE

Ha! I genuinely laughed out loud at the 'and don't get me started'. I imagine it being delivered by an old lord of the manor, dressed in tweed, leaning up against the fireplace, having one huge suck on his Sherlock Holmes pipe before fiercely turning around to camera to deliver 'and don't get me started'. Wasn't going to mate, chill out.

> *One of the most vague and verbose books I have ever read.*

I had to Google 'verbose', to be fair.

> *Absolute rubbish.*

Not very verbose.

> *I really didn't get on with this book. The font is obnoxiously large.*

Sorry.

> *200+ pages of tedious, rambling fluff and filler, and 51 that may be worth reading.*

51? Weirdly specific.

> *Not what I expected as i was expecting to be simple but NO!!! It is as if half of the book was wrote by a 15 year old Shakespeare!!*

a) 'written'

b) Your 'criticism' likens me to Shakespeare. Cheers!

So, if we genuinely try our best, should we fear criticism from others? Never! There's only one way to avoid criticism and that's to do nothing. Sorry, not an option. We've bills to pay and dogs to save!

So that's the 'fear of criticism' part knocked out of the definition park. What's next? 'Doubting your abilities and feeling like a fraud.' Feeling like a fraud? Try this event for size.

In 2005, Her Royal Highness the Princess Royal was set to visit the agricultural college in London where I used to lecture on the animal behaviour and husbandry course. I no longer taught there, but I rented one of their paddocks for my group classes and one-to-one training sessions. Although security was clearly going to be tight for the royal visit, the management at the college suggested it would be a nice addition to the festivities, plus a good photo op for the press, if I were to put on a dog training demo as the throng perused the site. Who knows, I might even get introduced to the top dog herself?

After resisting the urge to say 'thanks but no thanks', and in an effort to stay true to my 'if I don't do it, someone else will' mantra, I agreed to put on a show.

The plan was that I would be doing a round of agility training as the blue bloods passed by. Agility training is the kind of thing you see on TV or at a police dog

MAGGIE

demonstration where the dog does long jumps, clear jumps and maybe even goes up and down a seesaw. (A little tip for burglars fleeing a crime scene – don't make your escape over a seesaw, pursuit dogs are trained for that stuff.) The college principal (and as I type this I can't believe how stupid I was) proudly told me his dog Maggie went to agility every Thursday and had done so for years. I could see he was excited at the prospect of having her involved and he promised me she'd be perfect for the demo. I was happy to oblige.

Maggie was to be dropped off with me in the morning so we could become buddies and run a few practice laps of the course to make sure all was tickety-boo before the audience assembled. The appointed hour arrived but, despite our plan, there was no Maggie to be seen. The principal had been held up with some kind of emergency and with two hours to go, I was stood in an agility arena with half a dozen jumps, a tunnel, a seesaw and no dog. With a couple of minutes to go until the crowd appeared, the sweating principal sprinted in with Maggie in tow.

Maggie had three legs.

I quickly lowered the jumps and hid the see saw. Then I looked up to see half a dozen crew-cut gorilla-men in dark glasses talking into their sleeves. Clearly the royal party was on its way to observe our agility extravaganza, trailed by a couple of hundred eager onlookers, local news journalists and press photographers. I pretended not to notice any of this and attempted my first lap with Maggie.

ANOTHER DAY, ANOTHER COLLAR

'Maggie!' I cheerfully called as I headed towards the first jump clutching a piece of cheese the size of a bowling ball, yet apparently not big enough to move Maggie from the start line. I called and called, jumped up and down, promised her whatever she wanted but nope, nothing doing. As everyone approached with cameras waiting to be entertained, I couldn't have felt like more of a fraud. I decided to bail on the agility training, kneeled next to Maggie and started a grooming demonstration instead. What else could I do?!

As HRH stood chatting to her public, the principal tiptoed over to me and whispered, 'Hydrotherapy. Not agility. Maggie does *hydrotherapy* every Thursday. Sorry.'

I was then called over to the Princess Royal for the promised meet and greet. It was a nippy November afternoon and I was in my usual dog training regalia of waterproofs and walking boots. I humbly approached Her Royal Highness and offered out my hand to say hello. As I did so, the lace loop of my right walking boot somehow attached itself to the little metal hook on my left walking boot. The moment I felt the tautness downstairs, I knew I was a goner. My head bowed to the inevitable, but my body, God love it, stoically attempted to stay upright. As I continued my approach, my footsteps became shorter and shorter, faster and faster. As the upper part of my body leaned further forwards, the laces constricted my steps like a lasso tipping the rodeo calf. I was at a forty-five-degree angle by the time I reached the Princess Royal.

MAGGIE

My planned solemn nod and handshake morphed into a diving high five. I continued ten yards past her, where I hit the ground like a sack of spuds. But fear not, dear reader, any embarrassment was skilfully saved as I forward rolled, stood up, continued my tiny-stepped jog all the way to Heathrow Airport, where I changed my name, boarded an airplane and had a facelift. I write this from an undisclosed location in the Caribbean with my cringing toenails still lodged in the insoles of my waterproof boots.

But, wait a moment. Surely a fraud is someone who says they're someone they're not. My view is that if you say you're trying to be the best XYZ that you can be, and you genuinely *are* trying to be the best XYZ you can be, then no one can accuse you of being a fraud. If they *do* call you a fraud, they're accusing you of something that simply isn't true. You wouldn't be upset if someone accused you of having two heads or three legs (sorry, Maggie). You'd just continue about your day, trying to be the best you can with the materials and knowledge you have.

I think people often feel like a fraud when they compare their internal picture of themselves to an external picture of others. Images of others in your industry or social circle looking amazing and glamorous and faultless on Instagram can be a tough pill to swallow when you're tired and emotional, or when you've just had another prospective client say no, or your hair's a mess (tell me about it). But hang on a minute: you're competing and comparing on an uneven playing field. As you flick through your phone,

ANOTHER DAY, ANOTHER COLLAR

you're in the *now*, and you're pitching yourself against the glamorous photo on Instagram that isn't *their* now. That picture was taken yesterday. It was their sixth attempt and even then it was just the picture they hated the least. Don't imagine I share pictures of me with dogs on Instagram because I think the *dog* looks good. I guarantee any selfie you see of me on social media is at least the tenth attempt, and that in the previous nine I look like Gollum.

'Doubting your abilities and feeling like a fraud.' We can throw that in the bin if we avoid stating that we're 'the best' and instead state that we're 'trying to be the best we can be.'

Progress is the goal, not perfection.

Imagine being perfect. Or, worse still, *thinking* you're perfect at something. How boring. No more lands to conquer forced Alexander the Great to cry salt tears.

No matter what our profession, we should reframe doubting our abilities as acknowledging that we're not as good as we're going to be. We should all be in the position of feeling we're not as good as we're going to be, whatever it is we do. That's not boring. That's exciting.

I think imposter syndrome comes from being uncertain. Uncertainty comes from moving forward into new and therefore inevitably unknown territory. It comes from knowing that we don't yet know it all, and it's fuelled by the anxiety of potential criticism. The only way to remain certain is to be a know-it-all. Picture someone in your mind who is always certain of themselves and has no doubt in their own head that they're always right. Someone who believes there's no value in moving into uncertain territory. Someone like that would never have imposter syndrome.

But would you want to swap places with them?

Dogs are the best medicine for imposter syndrome. I think that's the reason I was always most comfortable in their company, be it at the track, in the street, at the community centre or in the back of my van at a security site. Dogs don't criticise. They take everyone at face value and they're brilliant at acknowledging good intentions. They're consistent, they're straightforward and if you're kind to them they'll be kind to you. We can learn a lot from that, about which communities we wish to immerse ourselves, and the type of people we want to be.

Lázaro

Let me tell you about the day I lost my religion.

It was 1983, I was twelve years old and the date was 1 April. A Friday. Good Friday, to be exact. I had been going to the local dog training club as a happy helper, without a dog of my own, for some time. At last, one of the owners asked me to do a private one-to-one training session with them and their dog. A real paid gig!

The dog in question was Honey, a beauty of a Shetland sheepdog, AKA a Sheltie. Honey lived with Peggy and Alan, who had been attending the club for a good few weeks. They asked me to do a session with them to teach Honey not to jump up at people. I asked Ron, the club's owner, if it was okay with him. Fair play, he knew how much it meant to me. 'If you're good enough, you're old enough, son. Go for it.'

Wow! My very first one-to-one dog training clients. With school about to break up for Easter, I agreed to meet the couple and Honey in the car park outside the clubhouse at 10am on Good Friday.

I planned the training session all week at school and each night in bed. I even rehearsed the phrases I would use to help establish my rightful role in society as a twelve-year-old dog training guru. Honey was a super friendly little dog. She just wanted to jump up to say hello to people. Unwittingly, those same people (including Peggy and Alan) had reinforced that behaviour by falling for Honey's sweet eyes and fussing her when her two feet were leaning on her victim's legs. I just had to put my big boy pants on and teach Honey (and Peggy and Alan!) that all the best fussing came when she had four feet on the floor.

When a behaviour recurs, something must be happening to reinforce it. Figuring out the behaviour we wanted to avoid was easy. Once Peggy and Alan appreciated what Honey expected as a result of jumping up (a fuss), all we had to do was figure out what behaviour we wanted instead (four feet on the floor) and to reinforce *that* position with a fuss instead. The hardest part, as always, was training the humans.

This ethos formed the backbone of my juvenile dog training lesson plans for the next decade or so. What is the unwanted behaviour? What is the behaviour's function from the dog's perspective? How is the behaviour working for the dog to make the dog want to keep on doing it? What alternative behaviour would we prefer? How can we offer reinforcement in exchange for that alternative behaviour? The dog gets what they want, the human gets what they want and I get what I want. ('That'll be £4 please, Peggy and Alan,' which by no coincidence was the entrance fee for the North Bank terrace at the Arsenal.)

Back to 1983 and, with a lesson in place in my head at least, I was in business.

Client booked? *Yep!*
Heart racing? *You betcha!*
Lesson plan? *Done!*
Date fixed? *Good Friday!*
Told all my mates I'll probably leave school early now that I've got a job? *Yep!*
Permission from Mum? *Er . . . nope!*

You know the movie scene when Dorothy goes from black-and-white Kansas into the Technicolor land of Oz? Well, Good Friday in our Irish Catholic home was just like that, but in reverse. Good Friday was the day when the colour drained. It meant no TV, no radio, no playing, no snacks, no dessert and definitely no going out dog training. I could hardly see through my tears as I walked with a hot five pence in my trembling fist to the telephone box a couple of streets from our home to call Peggy and Alan and tell them I had to postpone. No doubt they'd go to another trainer and I'd therefore have to work in a bank for the next fifty years.

I'll tell you what we *did* have on Good Friday, though. Church. Lots and lots of lovely church. Procession around the town behind the crucifix at nine in the morning, benediction at three in the afternoon and Stations of the Cross at half past seven. This was a service that focused on a series of fifteen individual images, distributed evenly up one side of the church and back down the other side, each depicting a chapter of Jesus's journey towards crucifixion and resurrection.

ANOTHER DAY, ANOTHER COLLAR

Obviously, nothing creates a hunger for TV and dog training more than not being allowed to watch TV or go dog training. Having survived what seemed like the first seventy-two hours of the sepia day holding back the tears from a combination of hangriness, no TV and missing out on my first, and what at the time I assumed was going to be my last, opportunity to be a professional dog trainer, my brother Anthony and I walked to the church to don our altar boys' cassocks and cottas (oh yeah, we were altar boys; 'course we were!) in time for 7.30 Stations of the Cross.

We sat in the sacristy waiting for the priest to arrive.

7.20pm

7.25pm

7.27pm

Anthony and I looked hopefully at each other. With only three minutes until kick-off, there was no sign of Father McMullen, who lived in a flat above the church. Things were looking up. Remember that feeling of hope at school when you had after-school detention and the teacher who dished out the penance forgot to turn up? That. Maybe Stations of the Cross was off?

But no such luck. Bang-bang, bang-bang. I heard the priest's footsteps thundering down the stairs and heading towards the sacristy. Our hearts sank. In dashed Father McMullen. 'Sorry I'm late, lads. I lost track of time. I've been watching *Chitty Chitty Bang Bang* and finishing off the Easter eggs!'

LÁZARO

What?

Not even 'eating' Easter eggs. *Finishing them off!*

I was raging. I'd endured this longest of holy days, this day of abstinence, this day where TV, Scooby snacks and dog training were forbidden, while Father McMullen, the actual priest, this holy man of God, was watching *Chitty Chitty Bang Bang* with his trotters up, munching on Switzerland's finest.

The scales, dear reader, fell from my eyes. I was twelve and everything was binary. You were in or out. *Swap Shop* or *Tiswas*. *Blue Peter* or *Magpie*. Arsenal or Spurs. Mod or casual. Heaven or hell. There was no in between. You couldn't have both. So, at the time, I decided to choose: dog or God?

Clearly I've made my bed, scratched it a bit, circled around inside it five or six times and slept in it. Amen.

Now I'm (nearly) a fully grown adult man, I'm not religious, but I'm as spiritual as the next shaman. I think we all are. You, me, our dogs. We're all designed to embrace the invitation to worship something and I think we are healthier when we do. I learned a bit more about worship when I was lucky enough to go to Peru in the early 2000s to study the dogs of Cusco.

Peruvians generally, and my tour guide Thiago specifically, worship Pachamama, or Mother Earth. Thiago was straight out of central casting. In his mid-thirties with a permanent smile and a genuine passion for sharing his love of Peru, he was the poster boy for trekking. I imagined that when he got home from work, he'd get changed out of his dusty North Face fleece and green cargo shorts into something more comfortable, like a less dusty North Face fleece and blue cargo shorts. Thiago shared my gratitude for being allowed to do lots of what we love. He would talk all day of the Peruvians' relationship with Mother Earth, with a special mention to the serpent, the puma and the condor. The serpent, he told me, was a symbol of wisdom, the puma an animal to inspire strength and integrity and the condor a link between heaven and earth.

Peru was invaded and colonised by the Spanish conquistadors in the sixteenth century. The Spanish brought Catholicism to the masses, building churches literally on the ruined ancient altars of the Incas. For example, the Spanish-built church of Santo Domingo in Cusco sits on top of, and cast into shadow forever, Coricancha, the Incan Temple of the Sun. Even now, however, the deity of Mother Earth maintains front and centre stage for many Peruvians. The trek we made to Machu Picchu, and the sunrise over the mystical ruins, was as spiritual as it gets. But move over Maharishi Judith Chalmers, let's get back to the dogs.

There's evidence that the Peruvians had a special relationship with their dogs long before the Spanish invaders arrived in the 1530s. In 2012, archaeologists unearthed in Lima the remains of ten dogs laid carefully and symmetrically in a resting position alongside the

LÁZARO

flanks of a woman, thought to have been buried around the year 900. Forty dogs buried a thousand years ago were discovered in 2006. The bodies had been carefully swaddled in blankets and each had been laid next to their own individual supply of treats: sustenance to get them through to the afterlife. As I learned during my visit, many indigenous people of the Andes believe that dogs chaperone the spirits of those humans who have died across the 'Dirty River', where they then meet a very special black dog, named Lázaro, whose role it is to lead the dearly departed safely over Achacaca, a bridge made of human hair (eeeew!), to meet their ancestors and live a happy ever afterlife.

The purpose of my trip to Peru, however, was to see what living dogs did there on a day-to-day basis, when given the choice.

Choice, or agency to make your own decisions, is a powerful reinforcer for learners. As I'm in the business of teaching owners and dogs, potential reinforcers are my stock in trade. The problem I have back home in the UK, however, is that we keep dogs safe in our homes, on leads and 'under control', so it's tricky to see what their genuine choices would be.

(Time out! I'm not suggesting we cut the shackles and release the hounds into the wild. It would be bedlam. Funny, but bedlam. Within a fortnight, German shepherds would be riding horseback and running the country.)

In Peru, and Cusco in particular, things are different.

ANOTHER DAY, ANOTHER COLLAR

Around 7am each morning, all of the front doors to the terraced cottages seemed to open at the same time like a sychronised advent calendar, and the dogs turfed out to go about their daily business. The dogs hook up with their other canine buddies and hang around all day. I'd follow these groups of dogs with my video camera and note how they would gather in small social groups, have a little sniff around and take a gentle mooch along to the main square, the Plaza de Armas, exploring a few bins along the way. At the main square, they'd chill with the tourists, have a good old nose around, watch the world go by and enjoy a large chunk of sun worshipping as they slabbed out on the lawns. These dogs had nothing specific to do and all day to do it. It was a special opportunity for me to witness what dogs would, given the choice, do all day.

Although the dogs generally hung around in loose but consistent social groups of four or five, I picked out one particular little black dog, nicknamed him Lázaro and decided to trace his steps. What would Lázaro choose to do?

He moved as if he had all the time in the world to explore his environment. No pressure. He seemed to be a nosy bugger. He enjoyed investigating the flowerbeds and park benches around the square. Of course, he loved to eat any snacks dropped on the ground by tourists and locals, and he seemed to worship the opportunity to be *with* the people in the square – not necessarily being cuddled or

LÁZARO

stroked, but just sitting next to humans or lying on the ground near them.

As I watched Lázaro satisfy his needs and wants, I meditated on my early days of training and my very first one-to-one training plan for Honey, which eventually I did get to put into practice with Peggy and Alan. Sure, addressing the function of any behaviour and how it gets reinforced or not is important. But just as important is that the dog in training is holistically content. Environment? Health? Diet? Exercise? Mental release? Problem-solving opportunities? Arousal? Gait? Relationships? The opportunity to worship something of value? All these considerations are equally important.

The dogs of Cusco were cool; they all pretty much had the same daily not-much-to-do list as my Lázaro. But I'll tell you what the dogs of Cuzco *didn't* do: they didn't bark, they didn't run and they didn't chase. These dogs had all day, no rush, no panic. No need to gorge. There were no dog fights or exaggerated signs of conflict. Off the lead, the dogs were able to communicate in subtler ways. Knowing that they had their flight option, they had no need to engage their fight option. At the end of the day, around 10pm, I'd follow them as they headed back to their individual family homes. The doors would open and the dogs would head on in for their bed and breakfast.

I followed these dogs for a week, not going back to my own hotel each night until I had watched from a distance little Lázaro safely ensconce himself back into his fire-lit

ANOTHER DAY, ANOTHER COLLAR

home, ready to go again tomorrow, and the next day. My heartfelt wish for him was that he would continue to have the opportunity to choose his own daily routine forever. For this life and the next.

Our dogs back home in the UK all have the same desires as the dogs of Cusco. However, due to our busy lifestyle and Western-world time pressures, if we're not careful, we can often feel that we have to cram a day's worth of canine nourishment into a half-hour dog walk. Owners rush to grab the lead and the dog, shoulder barge the front door open and *go go go!* The dog, eyes spinning and heart racing, feverishly sniffs and pulls, highly aroused as they head towards other dogs but are dragged away from much-needed same-species social interaction by their no-time-to-waste-need-to-get-on owner. 'Next time,' the owner says as they race back home, lock the dog in the house and crack on with their own busy schedule. The dog, however, still suffering from a frantic supermarket sweep of a walk, is left hanging. So much arousal and nowhere to put it, until tomorrow . . .

Trouble is, when things get too compressed, they eventually pop. If I were a pet dog who had the option to live either in Peru or in the UK, I know which location and lifestyle I'd opt for. So my advice for you and your dog is to simply slow down. Spend time with each other. Slow time. Learn from the dogs of Peru. They know the meaning of life. They've been doing it for long enough to be good at it. Imitate what they choose to do, given the choice. Take relaxed, social walks. Give them the opportunity to sniff slowly at their own pace, explore and discover. Give them time to worship each other, your lives and the environment around you. Don't pump in more adrenaline if you've nowhere constructive to put it. Instead, lie under a tree together in the sun and go to sleep. I bet you're both sun worshippers. And I know for a fact that, given the chance, your dog worships you and would love you to reciprocate.

I started this chapter having a dig at religion. I don't really mean to. I certainly don't want to cast shade on anyone's beliefs. I hope everyone has something or someone to worship, and I hope it adds value to their lives and encourages them to add value to the lives of others.

Personally, by appreciating Mother Earth in general and dogs in particular, I get to see, touch, smell and hear her miracles every day. It gives me energy. If I see a deer, a kestrel, a snake or a fox, I feel like I'm well in credit for the day. It warms my soul and makes me want to share that warmth.

If that's not religion, I don't know what is.

I love loving nature and my worship of animals. And although I'd be happy if it were purely altruistic, it's not. My love of dogs has given me a career and a life I could only dream of when I was a kid making plans for Honey. And now, as a born-again whatever, I get to watch

ANOTHER DAY, ANOTHER COLLAR

Chitty Chitty Bang Bang, train dogs and eat chocolate whenever I bloody well want to.

Thank Dog for that!

Over Land and Sea

China's a funny old place, let me tell you.

Several years ago, I was contacted by a couple of businessmen from Shanghai who wanted to develop the Chinese wing of my company, the Institute of Modern Dog Trainers.

The IMDT had its genesis one summer's evening back in 1999. I was teaching some clients how to turn your pet dog into a tracking dog. All of a sudden, the heavens opened and we took shelter in a barn. As pivots go, this was a good one, I started talking to the class about how dogs learn, classical conditioning, emotional responses and various dog training theories. By the end of the session, my clients were hungry for more. So I started to offer more and more courses and soon my client base evolved from those who wanted to be good dog owners into those who wanted to be good dog trainers. People from other dog training schools started sending their assistants to attend those courses, and it developed into something much more structured and formalised, with assessments and memberships and accreditations.

As the years passed, and my passion grew for teaching others to become dog trainers, and so improve the welfare of dogs worldwide, we expanded our institute into Australia and South Africa. I'd always been keen to develop the standard of dog training and behaviour in China, for several reasons. One reason is the size of the country. A one per cent improvement in welfare and training ethics for their dogs would be huge. Another is that I love exploring new cultures. A third reason is that I knew a lot of people would criticise me for wanting to go, and you know how I feel about critics! 'Yeah, but they eat dogs in China!' That was always the unimaginative opening barrage from the armchair critics. As far as I'm concerned, that's not a reason not to go, it's a massive reason *to* go. There are too many talkers and not enough doers.

The initial contact from China was so unexpected it felt too good to be true. When I received the first enquiry and a few follow-up emails, I decided to stress test it nice and early. I said I'd love to have a meeting to discuss the matter further, so why didn't they jump on a plane and fly over from Shanghai so we could have a meeting the following week at The Kings Head, a pub no more than 500 metres from my house?

They only bloody did!

Doers. Excellent!

We met at the pub (I walked there) and, with the niceties over, the two business guys told me how they were fans of IMDT and how they believed that with the backing of their money men and my experience of building education centres for dog trainers, the time was perfect to create CIMDT: the China Institute of Modern Dog Trainers.

When I first started teaching other dog trainers, necessity and finances dictated that those initial courses were somewhat on the cheap side. My classroom, believe it or not, was in the back of an old lorry. I could accommodate ten students, but they had to bring their own chair! Lighting came courtesy of nine extension cables plugged into a generator, which powered three bare light bulbs plus my old bedside lamp. As classrooms went, things were cosy, if not a little agricultural.

I didn't propose the back of a lorry to these businessmen from Shanghai. Instead, I suggested that they look into hiring lecture rooms in universities and colleges for us to present our courses. 'No, no, no, Mr Mann,' they said. 'We're not *hiring* you a college, we're *building* you a college.' They pulled out of their briefcases a series of plans for a four-storey building that they intended to construct in Shanghai for CIMDT, complete with a huge rooftop garden for our practical lessons with dogs.

My heart raced with the realisation that this was really going to happen. *Nice and cool*, I told myself. 'Good, that'll work,' I said, giving it large as if I wouldn't get out of bed for less.

Fast forward a few months, which included several visits to the Chinese embassy to sort out my work visa, and I'm on the plane to Shanghai. I absolutely adored the 'If we're going to do it, let's bloody do it!' aggression of the businessmen driving the project. I entered our new CIMDT building and it blew my socks off. They let me decide where the classrooms were to go, where the dogs could chill out, where we needed air con, the location of breakout rooms for students, the lot. The only thing they insisted on that I hadn't considered was a licensed bar for the students after class. Unorthodox, but who was I to argue? Meetings were held, plans were drawn up and the internal layout of the building was completed. The China Institute of Modern Dog Trainer courses are now presented in Shanghai to those who dream of becoming dog trainers and improving the training and welfare of dogs throughout the Far East.

When I first visited China, dog owners would say to me, 'We want to love our dogs, we just don't know how to.' It was such a sweet, innocent statement and really lit a fire under me.

In the West, we have a longstanding tradition of living with dogs as pets and valued family members. Quite frankly, I think some people in the UK find it easier to love their dogs than to love certain human family members! A while ago, I posted a question on Facebook: 'If you could ask your dog one question, and for one glorious minute your dog could answer you in English so you'd understand, what would you ask?' The vast majority of the hundreds of replies were from people dying to ask their dogs, 'Are you happy?' I followed it up with another question: 'How many of you ask your own family members "Are you happy?"' No one replied!

Our journey in the West from introduction to dogs to a symbiotic and loving relationship with them has been a nice gradual process that has served both parties well. Conversely, in China, it seems like the idea of owning pet dogs is new and unfamiliar, and they don't have the history and tradition to ease them into this new way of thinking. Even now, although the pointy end of my business in China is about developing canine training and behaviour education with accredited qualifications, the overriding mission statement for CIMDT remains: help people to learn the best way to love dogs. I honestly believe that if we love our dogs and our dogs love us, we're 99 per cent there, no matter where we are in the world.

I don't take for granted the overseas doors that being a dog trainer has opened for me. As part of the Institute of Modern Dog Trainers, I've been to so many amazing countries, and the education has most definitely cross-pollinated. Dog trainers are a funny old bunch, but as I've taught in so many different countries, I've formed a loose feel for each audience depending on where they are in the world.

In South Africa and Australia, for instance, the dog trainers always want me to 'tell it how it is'. There's no need to sugarcoat anything. If they're doing it wrong, tell them ASAP. There's not a lot of pearl-clutching in these countries either – I'd really have to go some to cause offence.

In Lithuania and Slovakia, the faces of many of the students suggest they've taken offence before I've even started teaching! Those Eastern Europeans make me work bloody hard before they're prepared to crack a smile. In Brazil and Fiji, however, it's all I can do to stop seminar attendees from permanently grinning!

ANOTHER DAY, ANOTHER COLLAR

When I first started presenting seminars and courses in Spain and Portugal, I really struggled with the relaxed pace. I'm used to cramming as much work into a day as possible, doing my talking while I'm walking, like the opening scene of a *West Wing* episode. Iberian dog trainers work at a very different cadence. I'd present an hour of a course, then we'd all head to a restaurant for three hours to chat about it. I'd be riddled with guilt for feeling that I wasn't covering enough ground, but eventually accepted that I was clearly being paid by the hour, not the mileage.

Ireland was a surprise when I first started teaching there. I assumed it was going to be #FierceCraic and, what with me being a plastic paddy myself, surely, we'd all be river dancing within minutes of each class starting. No such luck! The first time I taught in Dublin, I entered the lecture room and the attendees, maybe a hundred of them, were all sat bolt upright with their pens laid parallel to their pads on their desks, in silence. I think they all had their formal education heads on and, from what I hear, the school system in Ireland is traditionally pretty strict. Once we'd broken the ice, however, and everyone realised I was more Father Ted than Mother Superior, we were in business.

In Norway, the standards of dog training are already super high, so I really need to be on my game when I'm presenting out there. I like the attitude of my Norwegian course attendees. They take their time, measure twice and cut once. Scandinavians ask proper questions, wear proper outdoor dog training gear and have proper dogs to prove it.

The Middle East? Now that's a different kettle of fish. I've been invited to Bahrain on three different occasions by three separate parties. The first party had hired me in my role as an operational dog unit instructor. I flew over to help deliver some refresher training for a private security and detection dog handler team. For the second visit, I could afford to get out of my dusty combat trousers and tough-guy technical boots, as I'd been invited out by the staff of a crazily wealthy gentleman to help train his three golden retrievers. Each dog had their own carbon-copy scaled-down version of the owner's palace, down to the air conditioning, marble floors, fountains and replica statues. If the main house had it, the dogs' houses did too. (It reminded me of the conundrum I received in China: 'We want to love our dogs, we just don't know how to.')

During that trip, I was asked by the local animal welfare organisation to assess several dogs in their care and to do a Q&A for their volunteers and staff. I was of course delighted to do this. In Bahrain and throughout the Middle East, they have an issue with what they refer to as 'desert dogs'. Desert dogs aren't a breed as such. They're the consequence of European and American expats when they first went to the Middle East to develop the oil industry. They'd have a family dog while they were out there but sadly, after their two- or three-year stint earning their money, they'd leave and abandon the pet dog in the street to fend for themselves. These abandoned dogs became strays, met other strays and created several generations of street dogs, or, more specifically, desert dogs. Their starting point was the usual breeds we'd see at home, with the usual body language our pet dogs use to communicate with us monkeys to let us know that they're happy, sad and everything else in between. After a few generations of living out on the streets *alongside* humans rather than *with* humans, their body language became much more subtle, as they only had to communicate with each other. The problem the animal welfare organisation had observed involved new expat families discovering a pregnant desert dog out on the street and, with the best intentions, feeding her. Once the litter was born, the family would adopt one of the pups to be their new family pet. All would go swimmingly well for the first few weeks, but then the 'bites out of the blue' would start. The humans didn't have the skills to read, understand and respond appropriately to the dog's body language.

The dogs that we're accustomed to as pets – Labradors, spaniels and the like – leave us in no doubt about their feelings. If they're not happy, they spell it out to us by yawning, then blinking, then dropping their head, then tucking their tail, then curling their lip, then growling . . . and only then do they bite. They speak in broad, obvious cheers of delight or boos of displeasure, like a Victorian music hall audience. These desert dogs spoke in whispers, until they were forced to scream. They didn't oblige with so many amber lights, going instead from green to red in a flash in order to stay safe. And when that happened, they were dumped at the rescue centre.

The education programme we set up in Bahrain comprised a series of videos and handouts detailing the dogs' communication methods. These materials were used to educate the centre's staff and support prospective new owners in how to listen and respond appropriately to what the dog was saying, so everyone could feel safe and heard. It created a foundation for longer-lasting relationships to flourish.

My third and final invitation to Bahrain was from a company that asked me to present talks on dog training and behaviour. Bahrain is full of expats and there's not much in the way of nightlife. So when someone like me rolls into town to present a talk on, for example, canine body language at the local yacht club, it turns out that even if you don't have a dog, or you don't even *like* dogs, you'll still buy tickets and turn up.

I prepared, as instructed, a two-hour presentation on canine body language, a topic close to my heart because the more we understand dogs' body language, the more chance we've got of understanding what our dogs need from us. In the welcome email I received before travelling, I was told it would be quite a smart venue, so I made an effort with the attire by remembering to tuck my polo shirt into my jeans. Not enough effort, as it turned out, because

ANOTHER DAY, ANOTHER COLLAR

I arrived at the venue to find a champagne reception and black-tied meeters and greeters. There was a red carpet at the entrance to the venue, a journalist for a glamorous magazine and a photographer snapping the guests as they arrived. You know that feeling of turning up to school and slowly realising everyone else knew it was a special non-school-uniform day except you?

Inside, the room was made out like a nightclub: glitter ball, DJ, the lot. The organisers shared with me the full schedule of the evening. I'd honestly thought it would be just me and my laptop but no, first there was to be a five-course, silver-service meal, then a live band, and only then the big event. *Ladies and gentleman, now for the double act you've all been waiting for, all the way from the UK, it's Steve Mann and his Amazing PowerPoint!*

As the revellers sparked up their cigars and filled their port glasses, and the most expat covers band you could imagine finished rinsing any joy out of David Bowie's *Diamond Dogs*, I took to the stage to present a lifetime's worth of findings regarding canine body language to a pissed audience of over 300, most of whom by this stage didn't know one end of a dog from the other, let alone cared.

What a weird night that was, although, in hindsight, we made it fun. Everyone, including me, had a great time and, although I was booked to present for two hours, I ended up doing four. I've no idea what I spoke about for so long but, thankfully, I suspect no one else did either . . .

Asbo

I can't talk about a life spent with dogs without also talking about the pain of losing them. It's a tough conversation. I'm going to ease you into the topic by first telling you how joyous Asbo, my first Malinois, was.

Asbo was born in 2008 at one of the security dog kennels I used to teach at, and I loved him. I adore the Malinois. It is one of the four types of Belgian shepherds (the other three are the curly coated Laekenois, the black-coated Groenendael and the long-coated fawn or tan Tervueren). I'm all about the Malinois, a Ferrari of a dog and a breed that leaves nothing on the field after a day's work. Historically, the Belgian shepherd was a herding dog, but they pretty much excel at any job: security, detection, search and rescue, police, military, sports and cuddles. You name it, they'll go at it full bore and I love them for that.

With his mahogany brown coat and charcoal mask, Asbo was as beautiful on the outside as he was on the inside. As a pup, he would ride everywhere with me. Before and after each class I taught, he would come out of the van to train and play with me. We left the house together at 6am every morning with George Harrison's 'Here Comes the Sun' blasting on the stereo and we trusted every word of the lyrics. We returned home together each night only when we were satisfied. We ate together, worked together, played together, slept together and dreamed together.

One morning at my training field, when Asbo was about sixteen weeks old, he retrieved his toy and, as I took it from his mouth, he had the very slightest of wobbles, like one of his legs had gone weak, just for a second. I stopped and frowned, wondering if it was just my eyes playing tricks on me. I assumed they were, as moments later Abso was straight up in my face, smiling and waiting for his toy to be thrown again.

As the days went by, however, Asbo had some more odd little episodes. Sometimes he'd stumble ever so slightly during play, or he'd zone out for a split-second during training, which was so out of character for him as normally he'd hang on my every word, and I on his. I've no doubt that initially, I attempted to dismiss his little wobbles as a trick of the light, but in my heart I knew we were in trouble.

Days turned to weeks and, sadly, Asbo's episodes occurred more frequently and became longer in duration. What first started as a tiny freeze during play developed weeks later into a collapse and seizure each time he got excited. It was so strange: it only happed when he was happy or excited, and it only happened when he was with me. What could be crueller than being punished for feeling happy and excited together?

I spent every single penny I had, plus more, with specialist vets up and down the country to try to get Asbo well again, but I failed. It reached the point where we couldn't play together anymore because as soon as our arousal rose and joy began to seep through our veins, he'd collapse. After each episode, which now lasted between ten and twenty seconds, he'd get up from the ground, shake himself off, refocus on me and smile. 'Come on, Dad, why look so worried?' Asbo was ill, but he chose optimism.

Soon, Asbo would have to stay at home when I went to work. Even then it reached the point where he'd be so happy to see me when I returned that, despite his medication, he'd collapse. All I could do was hold him and cry as he shook each night. It destroyed me.

At the age of six months, Asbo collapsed for the last time in the kitchen and died in my arms. I collapsed too and held him for over three hours, sobbing. I refused to take my eyes from his chest, convincing myself that I could see him breathing, that he was just having another little wobble. But this time it really was just a trick of the light. There was to be no more 'Here Comes the Sun' as I drove to work in a much colder van after Asbo left us. 'All Things Must Pass' was the best I could hope for.

If you're a first-time owner or haven't yet had to go through losing a dog, take some advice from an old fool. I've learned to face up to most things in life that cause me upset or discomfort, to walk directly at the trigger to relieve the tension. If I have a horrible feeling of things slipping out of my control, I proactively head towards the issue to prove to myself that I will happen to life, rather than let uncontrollable life happen to me. It's an insecurity, but it's got me through a lot in the past. However, as a tool for dealing with death, it's useless.

Because death, and its snide shadow grief, definitely happen *to* us.

I'd love to give you the inside line here, but there's no hack for fast-tracking the grief of losing a dog. Having lost so many dogs over so many years, I've realised that the only thing I can do with grief is to recognise it – malignant intruder that it is – and to sit with it.

My heart was broken as I left the vet's surgery after dropping Asbo off to be cremated. I tried to swallow my anger through a constricted throat. I remember struggling to sign the paperwork at reception as I tried to balance the hot, barbed tears in my eyes, the same way I used to try and balance them on the school bus all those years ago. The receptionist spoke to me about urns as if they were important. Nothing was ever going to be important again. As I walked from the surgery out onto the busy high street, I felt like I was in a Radiohead music video, where the singer is stood dead still but everyone else is a busy blur, getting on with their lives, unaware that the saddest thing ever has just happened. I couldn't face going back home or to my colleagues. I'm not good with sympathy. I'm not a 'run free over the rainbow bridge' kind of guy. Instead, I drove to the field where Asbo and I used to train and play together. I climbed into the back of the van and fell asleep on his bedding with his toys. I cried my eyes out and I stayed there all day.

When I got home, I didn't feel any better, but I didn't feel any worse.

For me, this numbness continues for a couple of weeks after losing a dog. I don't register conversations. I don't taste food. I've no interest in music. I'm hollow. When I lost Asbo, I had to make a concerted effort to sit with the sadness. He was brave enough to choose his own attitude to his illness. I owed it to him to choose my own attitude to his death. He wouldn't have wanted it to be anger. I decided I would lean into every day optimistically, the way Asbo taught me to. Dogs know that you can't always control life but, if you watch them carefully, they'll show you every day how you can and should choose your own attitude.

Losing a dog is such a kick in the guts. Be ready for it and don't try to fight it. It's an invisible ten-storey-high opponent. People say grief is the price you pay for love. It's a painfully high price, but it's still an amazing deal.

Lucky

My dad wasn't one for giving advice. I'm not sure he thought it was his place. Clearly, this particular apple, when it fell from that particular tree, jumped onto the back of a stolen Del Monte lorry and now couldn't be further away if it tried. However, my dad did give me two pieces of advice in the only domain one male should ever offer another male counsel: association football.

I've already shared the first piece of advice with you: if you're going to do anything, try your best or not at all. I hope I've lived up to that, and always tried my best to do what I can for dogs. His second piece of advice was this: make your own luck.

As a kid, if I hit the crossbar when taking a penalty, I wasn't unlucky as far as Dad was concerned. His opinion was that I'd taken the opportunity to shoot the penalty, which was good. However, I hadn't prepared sufficiently to be accurate. 'The goal never moves,' he would say. If we conceded a goal in the final minute of the game, again, we weren't unlucky. It was simply a goal conceded during the match. It was no more or less lucky for the other team than if they had scored it in the first, thirtieth or fiftieth minute. The other team was simply mentally and physically prepared to keep attacking. They practised and were brave enough to take their opportunities.

Of course, we can be fortunate into which age, culture and family we're born. But as far as Dad was concerned, once we're no longer babies, we make our own luck. Because luck is where opportunity meets preparation.

We can choose to put ourselves in the right place to cross paths with opportunity. Sometimes, it's a difficult choice. We might have to choose not to go to a social event because a clashing business event could present an opportunity. We might have to get up earlier or travel further. We might have to stand up in front of others, even though we're buckled by anxiety because, if we don't, we won't be seen. We can choose to prepare well enough to have the skills to convert if and when the opportunity presents. Practise. Rehearse. Revise.

We also need to be prepared to take the opportunity. To be brave. To be prepared to fail. Failing is fine as long as it's with a clear conscience; you've tried your best and you learn from the outcome. 'Lucky' people tend to be those who regularly put themselves in areas where opportunities occur. They'll have done their preparation and will be brave enough to have a go.

So whether you're taking a last-minute penalty, building a career or starting a relationship, do everything you can to make your own luck.

These were the only two pieces of sage 'pull up a chair, son' pieces of advice I had from my dad. In fact, to illustrate his hesitancy for earnest conversation, read on.

But be warned – it's a bit earthy, so you may want to ask any kids or pups to leave the room.

It was a Saturday morning, I was thirteen years old and Dad was driving me home from football after a match. Rather than turning left off the main road into our street, he continued to drive straight on and pulled into the lane where he had an allotment. Turning off the engine and pulling the handbrake, eyes glued straight ahead through the windscreen, he swallowed hard. 'Your mother wants me to have a word with you,' he said. 'About, you know . . . the birds and the bees.'

Kill me now! I felt my ears go red and suddenly I realised that, just like him, I was also sat bolt upright and staring straight through the wind-screen. I prayed for a big Acme anvil to land on the car to put both of us out of our Irish Catholic misery.

Me: It's fine, Dad, there's no need. It's fine.

Dad: Your mother wants me to have a word.

Me: Honestly, Dad, you don't have to.

Dad: Well, I need to tell you . . . there's something you *shouldn't* do.

Me: I *know*, Dad, it's fine. Can we go now, please?

Dad: Well, what letter does it begin with?

Me: W!

And before I had even finished saying the letter W, Dad had pulled his seatbelt back on and started the engine. 'Grand!' he announced, and we were off home, never to discuss such matters again.

ANOTHER DAY, ANOTHER COLLAR

Despite Dad's unconscious attempt to poison football by pairing it with the most awkward conversation in the world, I still love football. And I *love* the Arsenal. I remember the very first time Dad took me to Highbury. It was November 1979 for a game against Everton. Nil–nil (cheers for that).

Dad's engrained desire to 'avoid any drama' meant that on match day we'd get to the stadium at least two hours before kick-off and would leave pretty much the same time as the caretaker was turning out the lights. I didn't care, though, I'd have lived there if I could. Walking from Finsbury Park tube station (two stops further away from Highbury stadium than necessary but, you know, 'avoid any drama'), we'd join the flow of freshly soaped honest working men walking faster than necessary, some with radios to their ears listening for team news and horse racing results, others more shifty, looking both ways and speaking over each other's shoulders in conspiratorial whispers, as Londoners do. I loved it.

That very first time, I remember walking up the dark internal stadium steps before stepping outside to see the hallowed turf of Highbury. I honestly thought there must have been lights under the grass, it was so bright. We were not only early enough to see the pre-warm-up, then the warm-up, then the match, we were there to see the nets being put up. We brought sandwiches! Who brings sandwiches to a football match?!

Once the crowd were in and the match kicked off, all

my senses, including my sense of belonging, were sparked. To this day, I still can't smell police horse dung and fried onions paired with an undercurrent of imminent violence without getting all Vera Lynn teary-eyed about it. I write these words having been at football last night (Arsenal vs Chelsea, 3–1 to Arsenal, thanks for asking) and of course it made me think about dog training, which ultimately/cripplingly/thankfully everything does in the end, including yoga.

There's a guy who stands behind me at the Arsenal, and I'm sure that in real life he's a perfectly nice chap. However, he only ever speaks to criticise. Arsenal could be winning 50–0 and he'd moan because it wasn't 51–0. There were three great goals last night, and all I heard from him were hollers of 'Wake up!' and 'What's that?' and the old seventies constructive classic: 'Rubbish!'

Now, I loved that game. And I don't look for, or scream at, the negatives like matey boy behind me. I do, however, go nuts when Arsenal score, far beyond what's reasonable. And therein lies the joy. I eagerly look for and comment when I see an Arsenal player pass well or bust a gut to win a fifty-fifty challenge. I know that even after a ninety minutes nil–nil, I'll have looked out for, seen and praised at least fifty things that made me happy. That'll put me in a particular mindset for the rest of the day, and it will positively affect those around me. Matey boy? No matter what the result, he'll have looked out for, seen and complained about at least fifty things he was unhappy about. That too will put him in a particular mindset for the rest of the day, which will negatively affect those around him.

What's more, how do you think the Arsenal players feel about what they hear? Who do they listen out for? Who best supports and encourages their efforts? Who do they want to please? Who do they want shouting on their sidelines? Who would they choose to ignore if they could?

It's the same with dog training.

When I was younger, the dog training classes I used to attend focused on 'corrections': choke chains, yanking on leads, loudly shouting, 'No!' All crummy, miserable ways to spend an hour with your dog. No matter what the dog did, the handlers were on the lookout for what was wrong, for behaviour that was not up to scratch, so they could spring into action and 'correct' it. I have no doubt what mood that owner left the class in, how the dog felt about the 'lesson', how the owner felt about the dog and how the dog felt about the owner.

We'll always see what we're looking for, and a fear of corrections breeds a fear of failure which breeds a fear of trying. My recommendation for you in dog training is that you look for behaviours you *do* want from your dog with a forensic intensity. It doesn't matter how small or even how sloppy they are. If your dog is optimistically having a go, your job is to grab that opportunity and celebrate it like you and your dog have just won the lottery. Guess what? If your dog's behaviour has earned them some positive feedback from you, and they like what they hear, then they're going to be prepared to have another go. And bingo, you get to spot it and reinforce it again. Now raise the bar – not too far – and with encouragement and an absence of the fear of failure, you'll be amazed at what you can achieve. Encourage your dog to try their best and to be *prepared* to grab any *opportunities* of positive reinforcement. Make your own luck and make them feel lucky to have you.

A final word about making your own luck. When I was a kid, my birthday 'present' each year was to get up at 5am on the closest Saturday to my birthday to go to work with my dad. We'd be the only ones 'working' at the Charringtons Brewery Depot in Mile End on a Saturday morning, where, as depot manager, he had to work when the place was empty at weekends. The sensory overload, coupled with the ungodly hour and the joy of it being my birthday present, made the brewery feel magical, like a boozy Willy Wonka's. I loved the smell of the old booze on the stained wooden brewery depot floor. I loved looking over the dock wall to see a million eels wrestling in the muddy Thames. I loved taking a spin on the forklift truck, weaving in and around the Tennent's Super beer barrels. And then, as the proverbial cherry on the metaphorical birthday cake, he'd take me to the greasy spoon café in Canning Town for breakfast. By this time is was about 8am, but I'd felt like I'd been up for at least forty hours.

I loved that café, full of cigarette smoke, swearing and copies of the *Racing Post*. When you ordered your breakfast from the Julie Goodyear-a-like behind the counter, she gave you a raffle ticket. You took your seat and eagerly waited for your number to be called from behind the hatch. 'Forty-two!' 'Forty-three, extra fried slice.' 'Forty-four! Forty-four? *Forrteeeeee fooouuurrrr!*'

Cholesterol bingo. Wonderful.

I cherished that father and son café time so much that I often repeated the ritual decades later with my own son, Luke, when he was a pup. On one such occasion, as we were leaving a lorry drivers' café, Luke, as all good five-year-old boys do, decided he needed a wee. And as all good five- to seventy-year-old boys do, he preferred the adventure of weeing outside up against a tree rather than in a formal water closet. Now, this café was in a big lorry park and behind it was a patch of scrubland, full of waist-high nettles and thistles. I stood with Luke as he splashed his Adidas Gazelles and, as I looked out into the wasteland, I saw, maybe fifty metres away, a brand new kettle barbecue grill slung into the nettles. It was still wrapped in clear plastic, its three legs stuck up in the air.

Not being one to want to miss an opportunity, and with summer just around the corner, I decided to head on in. 'Stay there, Luke,' I said as I pulled his shorts up and my sleeves down over my hands to minimise the nettle stings.

LUCKY

I ploughed in, 'effing and jeffing as I took jab after jab from the vegetation. Determined to get to my prize, I noticed as I got closer that it wasn't a kettle barbecue at all, but a kettle drum.

I hadn't seen a kettle drum since spotting one in the school pond. *Somebody* (the smart money that morning break suggested a disgruntled ex-pupil) had broken in during the summer holidays and lobbed every musical instrument into the pond. An ex-pupil clearly from the Chris Persimmon school of surrealism. Now, as I lifted the drum above my head to make my way out of the nettles, like Poseidon emerging heroically from the sea, what should I clock but another bloody kettle drum! Brand new, wrapped in plastic, teasing me.

I figured a weary lorry driver must have pulled into the lorry park for a kip at the end of a long day's delivering and, as he opened the doors to check it was empty, emitted a big old 'Oh, bugger!' as he realised he'd somehow missed an important delivery. Somewhere back on his route there must have been a gentleman in full black tie and tails standing on the pavement, tapping his watch and desperately looking up and down the avenue. I imagined the driver had muttered, 'Sod that!' and, rather than have to retrace his delivery route or admit his error back at the depot, pulled the drums off the lorry in the black of night and launched them into the nettles, never to be seen again. Or so he thought.

Having recovered the brace of timpani, I then had to

get them, and Luke, safely home. Into the dog van I dived. I pulled out every dog lead, tracking harness and collar I could find, attached them all together to give myself enough cordage to lash the two monster drums to the top of the van, and headed off home with my fingers crossed that we wouldn't be pulled over by the old Bill or, worse still, Phil Collins.

Back home, I took some photos and uploaded them to eBay. Hey presto, twenty-four hours later a chap from the Manchester Philharmonic had taken them off my hands, having greased my palm with a cool £1,200. That night, with my hat still at a jaunty angle from my win, I regaled the story to my mates Andy, Ken and José as we sat in the pub. 'That's ridiculous,' said José. 'You're so lucky.'

Ken then dropped a pearl of wisdom (what is it they say, even a stopped clock tells the right time twice a day?) 'To be fair,' he said, 'stuff like that happens to us all the time. But who of us other than Steve would bother to roll down his sleeves and tramp though waist-high thistles and nettles just to look at an old barbecue?'

Fair point.

It's not luck.

These opportunities are floating around us all the time. Sometimes we have to fight through the nettles to get at them. Those nettles might be trying to rebuild – physically and emotionally – a stray dog that's had an abusive start in life; or loving and losing a dog like Asbo; or not having money when your mates are in normal jobs and you're scratching around trying to make a living; or sleeping in the back of a van with a security dog while the rest of the world's tucked up safe and sound under the duvet.

Sometimes those nettles really hurt, but it's up to us to choose our own attitude and decide if we're prepared to go through them or not.

Timing

As B. F. Skinner almost said, the dog is always right. I've also noticed that the dog always seems to arrive at the right time in life.

My grandad's dog Buff timed his run so perfectly that he helped me associate being with a dog with everything that was wonderful in my life at the time: youth, long summer holidays, absence from school, sun, Ireland, family and freedom. My happiness became anchored to, and reliant on, the presence of dogs. Despite my prayers and begging, no dog arrived for me at home back in the UK when I was a kid. That absence created a scarcity, a hunger and a desire so strong that when I finally did manage to snare my own dog, the bond was irreversible and would dictate the trajectory of the rest of my life.

A dog named 'Dog' bounded into our junior school playground (albeit with the assistance of Chris Persimmon) to show me that no matter how miserable the environment, a dog will always have the ability to make me smile. And if I can smile, I can do anything.

Banjo, the hardcore kelpie I watched in wonder as he worked the livestock out in Australia, came at just the right time in my life to show me how he wasn't wired even to consider what he'd do if he failed to move the bull. His job was to move the bull so move the bull he would.

ANOTHER DAY, ANOTHER COLLAR

He taught me that if you feel born to do a particular job, you should do that job.

Pele the greyhound came to me at a time in my life when I needed a mentor to show me how to chase and commit. No half measures. All or nothing. Commit to chasing 100 per cent and you won't even see the others racing around you, let alone hear their criticism. If you're running, run 100 per cent, like your life depends on it. If you're lounging, melt into that settee forever. And if you want something in life, like bread, grab it.

My adorable Nancy landed with me at a time when I needed to learn to look at life from the perspective of others. The tunnel vision lessons taught to me by Pele were necessary to get me into position, but when left unchecked such drive can become unhealthy and selfish to those around you. Nancy, tiny little Nancy, forced me to look at the world from her perspective. A tiny dog struggling in the land of giants needed empathy and a bespoke care plan. She showed me that when we finally feel safe, secure and loved, we no longer have to keep running.

Chump arrived at a time to show me that anyone and everyone can star in their own movie if they choose to. When Chump's kennel door was opened by Selina at the rescue centre, he bravely marched out and never looked back. Having been part of the winning team with Chump on *The Underdog Show*, I was encouraged to set up the Institute of Modern Dog Trainers to open the kennel door

TIMING

for as many people as possible who wanted to become accredited positive dog trainers. It's a family that continues to grow and that I adore.

Three-legged Maggie sneaked up on me during a period in which I was sensitive and afraid of being caught out as a fraud, an imposter. Maggie reiterated to me that life really isn't about the survival of the fittest, or even the best. Life's about survival of the most adaptable and those who genuinely try their best.

'Mad' Max entered my life at the perfect time to hold a mirror up to my unsustainable work regime. To tell me to slow down, take a breath and to look after my tools. If we don't really care for our health, exercise and sleep then, hand on heart, we don't really care enough.

Honey, Itzy and Teddy arrived to show me that dogs will always be prepared to teach us when we're prepared to listen.

Asbo taught me perhaps the most valuable lesson possible: that no matter what happens, you always get to choose your own attitude.

And then there's Alfa. My perfect Alfa. Much like Lázaro in Peru leads the departed from this world into the next world of paradise, Alfa was sent to guide me from my mundane life into a paradise of working with dogs. He taught me that a dog's lessons last forever. And he taught me that being funny, handsome and humble really helps!!

ANOTHER DAY, ANOTHER COLLAR

When I was seven, I was desperate to have my own dog, so my mum and dad got me a hamster.

Unsurprisingly, that wasn't enough, so I'd spend every hour I could playing out in the street with the dogs of our neighbours.

But that wasn't enough, so when aged eight I saw on the church noticeboard that a dog training school was opening at our local community centre, I went along without a dog.

But that wasn't enough, so I would beg, borrow or steal a dog every Thursday evening to take to dog training school

But that wasn't enough, so I would get there early to help set up the classes, put out the cones, mop the floor, make the tea, listen and smile.

But that wasn't enough, so I started to assist in the classes, demonstrations and exercises, and do a little one-to-one training.

But that wasn't enough, so I set up my own classes, evenings and weekends, to reach more dogs.

But that wasn't enough, so I started travelling around the country to watch and teach at other clubs to reach more dogs.

But that wasn't enough, so I helped other trainers set up their own classes too, to reach more dogs.

But that wasn't enough, so I set up the Institute of Modern Dog Trainers, to formally teach and qualify new trainers and enable them to go out and reach more dogs throughout the UK and Ireland.

TIMING

But that wasn't enough, so I set up the Institute of Modern Dog Trainers in Australia, South Africa and China to reach more dogs.

But that wasn't enough, so I wrote some dog training books to reach more dogs.

But that wasn't enough, so I wrote this book.

And you know what? This won't be enough either. I want to reach every single dog in the world to try to make their lives better. To return the favour.

My journey hasn't been in a straight line. It has been riddled with mistakes, but I've always tried my best. I've never relied on luck and I've been taught a lesson every day by a dog. Although at times I could have blamed the barriers to being a dog trainer on others, the responsibility to smash those barriers has always been mine.

Whatever happens, I'm never going to reach enough dogs.

But if I ever do, I'm going to start all over again, this time with cats.

Acknowledgements

I'd like to thank Matthew Phillips and Lucy Tirahan of Bonnier Books UK for their support in bringing this book to life. Merci to Adam Parfitt for helping me rearrange my alphabetti spaghetti and gracias to Martin Roach for introducing me to the world of book writing, you owe me!

When it comes down to it, it's all about the dogs really, isn't it? I'm forever grateful for all of the beautiful, wise, funny, motivating and comforting dogs that have crossed my path in the past, and I'm excited for all of those I'm going to get to hang out with in the future.

Be as kind as you possibly can to every dog you meet, I think it's the meaning of life.

Finally, I'd like to acknowledge every single person that suggested this book should be called *Mann's Best Friend*. C'mon, you're better than that.

EVEN MORE FROM THE UK'S NO.1 DOG TRAINER

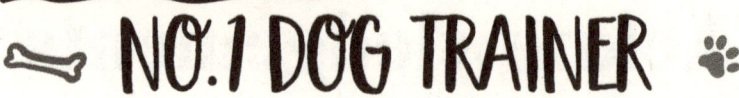

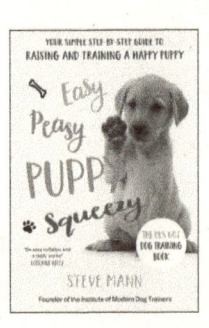

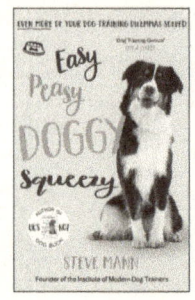

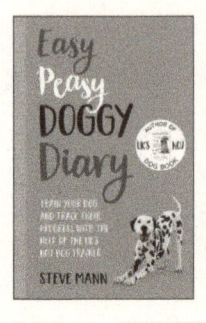

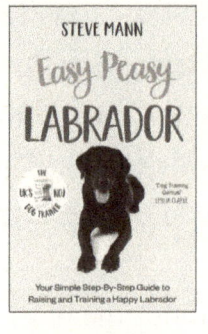

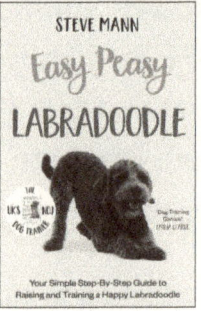

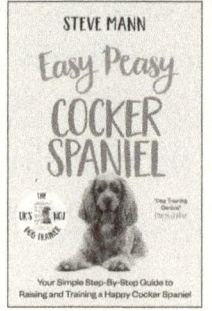

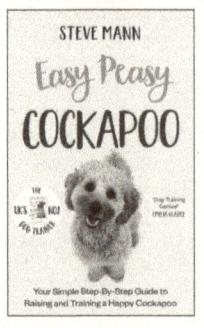